Jesus' Sheep

A Look at the Behaviors of God's People and Why We All Need a Good Shepherd

Jeff Gwaltney

© **Copyright 2024 - All rights reserved.**

The content contained within this book may not be reproduced, duplicated or transmitted without direct written permission from the author or the publisher.

Under no circumstances will any blame or legal responsibility be held against the publisher, or author, for any damages, reparation, or monetary loss due to the information contained within this book, either directly or indirectly.

Legal Notice:

This book is copyright protected. It is only for personal use. You cannot amend, distribute, sell, use, quote or paraphrase any part, or the content within this book, without the consent of the author or publisher.

Disclaimer Notice:

Please note the information contained within this document is for educational and entertainment purposes only. All effort has been executed to present accurate, up to date, reliable, complete information. No warranties of any kind are declared or implied. Readers acknowledge that the author is not engaged in the rendering of legal, financial, medical or professional advice. The content within this book has been derived from various sources. Please consult a licensed professional before attempting any techniques outlined in this book.

By reading this document, the reader agrees that under no circumstances is the author responsible for any losses, direct or indirect, that are incurred as a result of the use of the information contained within this document, including, but not limited to, errors, omissions, or inaccuracies.

Dedication

To my beautiful wife and children. Thank you for being the inspiration and love of my life.

Table of Contents

FOREWORD 1

INTRODUCTION 3

CHAPTER 1: JESUS AS THE GOOD SHEPHERD 7
   SHEPHERDING FROM GENESIS TO REVELATION 8
   THE QUALITIES OF THE GOOD SHEPHERD 10
      The Good Shepherd Lays Down His Life for Us 11
      The Good Shepherd Provides for Us 12
      The Good Shepherd Guides Us 14
      The Good Shepherd Unites Us 15
      The Good Shepherd Loves Us 15
      The Good Shepherd Knows Us 17
      The Good Shepherd Keeps Us Safe 17

CHAPTER 2: THE SHEEP'S POSTURE 19
   SHEEP BEHAVIORS 20
   SHEEP CHARACTERISTICS 21
   PEOPLE OF GOD: THE SHEEP OF HIS PASTURE 22

CHAPTER 3: JESUS' SHEEP—FOLLOW 25
   WHY FOLLOW THE GOOD SHEPHERD? 26
      Because He Leads 27
      Because He Saves 28
      Because He Gives Abundant Life 29
      Because He Cares 29
   FOLLOW THE GOOD SHEPHERD: IT IS NOT A CONTEST, BUT A RELATIONSHIP 30
   HOW TO FOLLOW THE GOOD SHEPHERD 33
      Believe in Jesus and Understand He Is God 34
      Foster a Personal Relationship With Him 35
      Know His Voice 35
      Stay in Church 36
      Walk in Purpose 38
      Diligently Seek Him 38
      Have a Heart of Gratitude 39
      Go Into the World and Share the Good News 39
      Stay Prayerful 40

CHAPTER 4: JESUS' SHEEP—STRAY 41

WHY DO WE STRAY? 41
- Sin 42
- Feelings 43
- Not Knowing What We Seek 44
- Finding Alternative Sources 45

RETURNING TO THE GOOD SHEPHERD 47
- Choose to Return 47
- Choose Repentance 49

ENCOUNTER THE GOOD SHEPHERD IN LOW MOMENTS 50
- Remember Where You Come From 51
- Identify and Address the Root of Straying 52
- Remember, His Presence Is Always With You 53
- Consider the Joy of Your Return 53

CHAPTER 5: JESUS' SHEEP—SLEEP 57

WHEN SLEEP ENDANGERS THE MISSION 59
HOW TO REMAIN AWAKE FOR THE MISSION 61
- Deny Selfish Ambition: Align Yourself to God's Will 62
- Practice Self-Control Not to Fall Into Temptation 63
- Keep Your Eyes Open and Stay Watchful 64
- Remember His Power at Work in You 66
- Have the Mindset Christ Had in Gethsemane 67

CHAPTER 6: JESUS' SHEEP—RUN 71

WHY RUN? 72
- A Bitter, Unforgiving Heart 73
- Living in Sin 74

THE TRUTH ABOUT RUNNING 76
- When We Run, God Is With Us Wherever We Are 77
- When We Run, God Pursues Us 77
- When We Run, God Interrupts Our Plans 78
- When We Run, the Storm Gets Worse 79

THE GOOD SHEPHERD PRESERVES 80
FEAR: A BARRIER TO OBEDIENCE 82
THE LORD SENT THAT 83
THE WINDOW OF CHANGE 85

CHAPTER 7: JESUS' SHEEP—FALL 87

THE SHEPHERD'S GOODNESS WHEN WE FALL 88
OUR FALL IS NOT FAILURE 89
- Falling Is Not Failure, It's Preparation 89
- Falling Is Not Failure, It's a Chance to Practice Humility 90

- *Falling Is Not Failure, It Exposes Our Need for Salvation* 92
- *Falling Is Not Failure, It Builds Our Faith* 92
- *Falling Is Not Failure, It's a Chance for Forgiveness* 94
- *Falling Is Not Failure, It's God's Pruning Process* 95
- NOT IF, BUT WHEN WE FALL 96
  - *The Fall Reveals Our Need for God* 97
  - *The Fall Teaches Us to Depend on the Good Shepherd* 98
- THE GOOD SHEPHERD RESPONDS WHEN WE FALL 99
  - *Jesus Lifts Us Up and Out* 100

CHAPTER 8: JESUS' SHEEP—FOUND 103

- TO BE FOUND IN JESUS CHRIST 104
  - *We Are Found in Jesus: Let's Unpack This* 105
- THE GOOD SHEPHERD IS PERSONAL 106
  - *A Closer Look Into Intimacy With the Good Shepherd* 107
- A PROMISE OF ETERNAL LIFE 108
- YOU NEED TO MAKE A DECISION TO LET THE GOOD SHEPHERD INTO YOUR HEART 110
  - *Decide to Turn to the Good Shepherd* 112
  - *Decide to Surrender to the Good Shepherd* 113
  - *Decide to Trust the Good Shepherd* 113
  - *Decide to Declare the Good Shepherd's Name—Jesus Christ* 114
  - *Decide to Approach Life With Truth and Compassion* 115
  - *Decide to Embrace the Good Shepherd's Gift of Grace and Freedom* 115
- STAY CONNECTED 116

CHAPTER 9: DAILY LIVING—WALKING WITH THE SHEPHERD 119

- PRACTICAL WAYS TO FOLLOW THE SHEPHERD 120
  - *Start and End Each Day in Prayer* 120
  - *Choose Your Company Wisely* 121
  - *Create Spiritual Boundaries* 121
  - *Submission or Surrender* 122
  - *Analyze Your Choices and Repent When You've Fallen Short* 123
- HOW TO REJOIN THE FLOCK AFTER STRAYING 124
  - *Find Community: Flock Are in Danger When Scattered* 124
  - *Get Close to the Shepherd Through the Bible (SOAP Method)* 125
  - *Make Time for Jesus in Solitude* 126
  - *Be Persistent and Patient With Yourself* 127
- WAKE UP FROM YOUR SLEEP 129
  - *Return to Wonder* 130
  - *Approach Prayer as a Chance to Talk to God* 130
  - *Ask the Holy Spirit for Restoration* 131
  - *Be Proactive, Not Passive* 131
- DAILY DEVOTIONALS TO RETURN AFTER RUNNING AWAY 132
  - *Run Back to Jesus* 132

How to Get Up When You Fall 137
   Pray With Purpose *137*
   Praise God *139*
You Are Found in Christ 140
   Reflect on God's Promises *140*
   Rely on God *141*

CONCLUSION 147

ABOUT THE AUTHOR 151

REFERENCES 153

Foreword

A pastor recently pointed out to me that the contemporary Western world does not fully grasp the significance of sheep and shepherd imagery in scripture. This observation holds true; modern industry and technology have shifted popular culture so far from the ancient, agriculture-driven world that we have lost the depth of biblical teachings centered around farming.

The terms "sheep" and "shepherd" carry profound meaning when understood in the context of our spiritual journey. The imagery of the Good Shepherd and His flock is rooted in an ancient agricultural framework, yet it conveys timeless truths about human vulnerability, divine care, and the unbreakable bond between the Shepherd and sheep.

This book offers hope and reassurance in a post-COVID-19 world marked by uncertainty, fear, and isolation. It invites us to see ourselves through the eyes of the Good Shepherd—precious, valued, and deeply loved. As the author skillfully draws us into the analogy of sheep and their shepherd, we are reminded of a God who not only watches over us but also actively seeks us when we stray.

The beauty of this book lies in what I refer to as profound simplicity. It speaks to both seasoned believers and seekers, breaking down complex theological truths into relatable concepts. From understanding the behavior of sheep to exploring transformative Bible study methods like SOAP and ACTS, this book provides practical insights. It encourages readers to draw closer to Christ, not out of fear or obligation but from a place of love, gratitude, and trust.

This book is about grace! We cannot fall from grace; we fall into its arms. Grace welcomes the wandering sheep and empowers us to follow the Shepherd more faithfully.

Through relatable examples and heartfelt reflections, Jeff Gwaltney portrays a God who guides, protects, and desires an intimate relationship with His sheep.

As you read this book, prepare for a journey of self-discovery and spiritual growth. Whether you are new to the faith or seeking a deeper walk with Jesus, this book will meet you where you are and gently guide you toward the abundant life promised by the Good Shepherd.

Open your heart and prepare to encounter the Shepherd in new or renewed ways. This book is more than just a text; it's an invitation to a life-transforming relationship with the One who calls you His own.

Antipas L. Harris, Ph.D., D.Min.

Introduction

You are probably thinking: *Shouldn't a book about shepherds and sheep be in the agricultural aisle of the store?* Well, I'm here to ease your mind. This book is not about farming. Yes, we talk about the Good Shepherd and His flock, but it has nothing to do with the actual farm life. After all, you can watch the Discovery Channel or YouTube for details on farming.

Think of this book as one massive but simple analogy to help you reframe how you see God. This will give you a better understanding of how valuable you are to him. So relax into your chair and get ready for a life-changing experience.

Have you ever driven past a countryside filled with gazing sheep? If not, I'm sure you've watched enough movies to imagine what that image is like. Sheep that are placed in a secure fenced area and allowed to roam freely within those parameters tend to appear more at ease, knowing that they are safe within the gates prepared by their shepherd.

On the other hand, a flock of sheep that is outside of the parameter tends to be anxiety-prone as they graze. This is because those outside the gates are alert to the possibility of danger lurking nearby. Sheep that graze without the protection or watchful eye of the shepherd are likely to leave the countryside and wander into the city, where they could be hit by cars, fall into unforeseen ditches, or get lost.

Much like the sheep in the example above, we are within the gates of safe grazing when we are in Christ. However, that change and danger have become more of our reality. While the sheep within the gate know how dangerous the world can be, they are at peace, trusting that the shepherd is taking care of it all for them. But sheep outside of the shepherd's protection are on guard, as they are burdened with the reality of having to fend for themselves. Sheep are helpless without a shepherd, both in real life and spiritually. As physical sheep struggle to survive without the protection and guidance of a shepherd, people are likened to sheep. We cannot make it through the tests of life without Jesus—our Good Shepherd. Like sheep, we are totally reliant on the Good Shepherd's protection and direction for our well-being. Essentially, we lack sound minds, good eyesight, and proper hearing when we live outside of Christ. We are also slow to escape the traps of this world and the predators who are constantly seeking to destroy us. Sheep have no claws, sharp hooves, or deadly jaws to defend themselves, so they easily become prey to animals in the wild. Likewise, without Jesus, we are defenseless—no camouflage or weapons for protection.

Friends, the Lord is your Good Shepherd as much as He is mine. He doesn't want us to be like those sheep who live a life of fear instead of faith. Jesus wants us to graze and roam freely, away from danger, within the gate He has provided for us. That's where the Bible and fellowship with people who encourage our faith come in. That's right. Whether you are in Christ or are yet to know Him, the Lord is *your* Shepherd, too. He personally longs to know and protect you.

The beauty of the Gospel is that the Lord loves us all equally, even when we leave the gate sometimes. So we can draw nearer to the Good Shepherd as His sheep without fear of judgment or being cast away. Jesus loves those who are curious about Him but don't know Him yet, just as much as He does those who are already in fellowship with Him.

Perhaps learning about the different behaviors of Jesus' sheep will help you come closer to Him. It will help you see that God expects your mistakes and shortcomings because He made you and loves you just the same. In this book, you'll better understand the Good Shepherd's love for His sheep. You'll see how personal our relationship with Jesus is and how much He has done to create a path for us to freely access Him.

This book also explores some fun methods you can use during Bible study and prayer to develop true intimacy with Jesus. It includes the scripture, observation, application, and prayer (SOAP) method, as well as the adoration, confession, thanksgiving, and supplication (ACTS) method for approaching quiet time with God. In these pages, you'll discover ways to follow the Good Shepherd, return to Him after straying, awaken your spirit, stand in Christ after falling, and be found in Him. We'll start with a deep dive into the idea of being sheep who follow the Good Shepherd so you can strengthen your faith or begin to structure it in Jesus. With this book, you'll broaden your knowledge of who Jesus is as your personal shepherd, why He is good, and why you need His mighty guidance and instruction.

Then, we'll explore reasons we are likened to sheep by understanding some of the behaviors we are prone to. Being referred to as sheep in the Bible is a term of endearment, unlike how someone would receive it as an insult from fleshly understanding. We are likened to sheep because of our need for sustenance, protection, direction, and much more—all of which are given by the Good Shepherd.

We are all sheep in need of a Good Shepherd to guide and shield us. Brace yourself. This book is about to deliver a transformative and informative message. By the end of it, you'll learn to forgive, show compassion, and continuously come to God with a repentant heart. It doesn't matter how many mistakes you make; the Good Shepherd never stops loving you. This is an opportunity to continue to build intimacy with Jesus. And if you find yourself lost and wandering, it is a chance to return to Him. The sheep we speak of in this book are you and me—people who need Jesus, our Good Shepherd, to receive eternal life.

Chapter 1:

Jesus as the Good Shepherd

Jesus' goodness separates Him from the world because He is the Good Shepherd. His goodness is distinguished by His undeniable nobility and praiseworthiness as God. He is the Good Shepherd because He claims His sheep as His own. No matter how messy we are or how far we stray from His instructions, He stands by His decision to love us.

Jesus is also the Good Shepherd because He is greatly concerned about us. God cares so much that He came to earth in the form of flesh as our Messiah so we may have a way to be rescued from the trespasses of our sin. No other shepherd is that good. Not even friends or close family would be willing to demonstrate their love through sacrificing themselves on the cross the way Jesus did.

The kind of concern and loving-kindness Jesus shows to us is unparalleled by anything we could ever experience. We should not take His goodness toward us for granted. The Good Shepherd left His own comfort for the sake of His sheep—how many can we say have ever, or would ever, do that? This type of love is only possible with and through God.

The Bible constantly emphasizes God's love and goodness, and that is not accidental. The theme recurs to remind us of who God says He is. His consistent nature makes it impossible to hide how good He is from the beginning to the end of the Holy text.

The Good Shepherd's concern for His sheep is evident in the Old Testament, when God personally intercedes and chooses David as king to lead Israel after Saul's massive disappointments. For context, you can refer to 1 Samuel 8. God's willingness to help His people when they ask for guidance has never faltered. We see His faithfulness again in the New Testament when Jesus is born in a manger on a mission to be the ultimate sacrifice for our sins **(refer to 1 Timothy 1:15–16)**.

Again, God was showing His care for us as His children. The point of these brief examples is that God's faithfulness has always remained unspoken, so much so that we can look to Jesus as our Good Shepherd daily. With that said, let's explore more about what it means for Jesus to be so good to us. We'll also explore the concept of shepherding from Genesis to Revelation so we can deepen our understanding of Jesus as our Good Shepherd.

Shepherding From Genesis to Revelation

The image of God as the Good Shepherd is conveyed throughout the Bible. In **Genesis 48:15**, when Jacob, the father of Joseph, was ill and on his deathbed, he proclaimed God as his shepherd all the days of his life (**Gladwell, n.d.**). Using his final strength, Jacob shared how God's faithfulness had carried him and guided him this far. That's who God is—a Good Shepherd with us from the very beginning of Genesis.

Jesus' story of being the Good Shepherd is found in the middle and extends to the last book of the Bible, declaring, "For the Lamb at the center of the throne will be their shepherd; 'he will lead them to springs of living water.' 'And God will wipe away every tear from their eyes'" (*The Holy Bible, New International Version,* 2011/1973, **Revelation 7:17**).

Shepherding has been a prominent theme throughout Scripture for so long that God even expressed strong words of rebuke for some of the bad shepherds in the Old Testament. From the very beginning, the Bible prophesies of a Good Shepherd (Jesus) who is yet to come. We see the New Testament reveal itself as a fulfillment of this prophecy as Jesus not only identifies Himself as our Lord and Messiah but also "the Good Shepherd" (*The Holy Bible, New International Version,* **2011/1973, John 10:11**).

A lot of the time, the idea of shepherding, especially that which is good, is applied to church leaders (**Gladwell, n.d.**). Shepherding appears frequently throughout the Bible, significantly pointing to Jesus as the Good Shepherd from whom others should learn.

The nature of the Good Shepherd is crucial to God's people, and the Bible emphasizes our need to recognize this. It can be said that God chose the notion of the Good Shepherd because we are prone to act like sheep. In that, we follow, stray or wander, sleep, run, and fall. Instagram is proof of the first point. People are prone to follow and avidly believe in something or someone. We click the "follow" button on Instagram to validate the next person and show that we are interested in their content. The same is true when we "follow" and "subscribe" to YouTube channels. Following is a fundamental part of human nature, and social media reflects our susceptibility to that behavior.

Also, we are prone to stray. It's rare to find someone who stays in one place from Monday to Friday. We move around for work and other responsibilities. Even those who work from home will need to leave the house for something at some point. How often do we set out on a mission to go to one place but veer off to various other places? Well, it's human nature to stray or get distracted from the primary goal. We can leave home on our way to a friend's house and decide to make a "quick stop" somewhere unplanned first. Sure, this is a very basic example, but it demonstrates how vulnerable human beings are to straying or veering off an intended path.

Perhaps a better example can be someone who starts off college studying medicine and then decides to drop that subject to take up another. We are prone to changing our minds, going off course, choosing different, and drifting outside the initial plan.

Don't get me started on sleep. Unlike God, Who doesn't slumber, many of us can sleep at night and find reasons to nap during the day. Of course, people need sleep to function daily, so it's an inevitable part of who we are.

We also run from problems, difficult conversations, and sometimes healthy relationships. What I've noticed is that people can willingly run toward what's not good for them because it's a temporary fix for joy. That's why we need the Good Shepherd to keep us on track and following the right path. He catches us whenever we fall, too. Because we are prone to behaving like sheep, the analogy of the Good Shepherd and His flock seems fitting.

Shepherding is essential because of our sheep-like behavior. God recognized from the beginning, when He made the first human beings, that without a compass to follow in the form of Jesus, the Good Shepherd, we would land ourselves in destructive territory. As such, we can fall into a place where we do things that are sinful and outside of His purpose for us. It is clear how helpless we are without a shepherd, so God made a way for us, and His name is Jesus.

The Qualities of the Good Shepherd

Jesus is the God of a gigantic, detailed universe, yet He is still concerned about us in every minor detail. The Bible tells us that we are so precious to the Good Shepherd that He numbers every hair on our head and calls us worthy (*The Holy Bible, New International Version,* **2011/1973, Luke 12:7**). The Good Shepherd is all-knowing, and yet He doesn't allow this to get in the way of intricately knowing His sheep.

Ezekiel 34:1–6 paints a picture of bad shepherds, leaders who slaughtered their sheep for personal gain and failed to provide for them to feed themselves. We see today's leaders and people in positions of power take advantage of being shepherds as greed and selfishness replace empathy. However, the Good Shepherd does the opposite of what's described in the book of Ezekiel. That's because God genuinely cares.

Instead of taking from us for personal gain, He gives us life and chances and even caters for our needs. The Good Shepherd is compassionate and shows concern for His sheep. He provides for us in ways that nourish, help, instruct, and free us. **Psalm 23:3** conveys that the Good Shepherd "restores" our soul for His name's sake, meaning knowing Jesus heals and allows us to rest in Him.

The Good Shepherd guides His sheep as He leads the way. He is intimately and intentionally involved with His flock and wants a relationship with us. Jesus cares for each person's safety, so much so that He willingly sacrificed His own comfort and life by coming to earth to die for the sake of His sheep. He loves us so much; He willingly gives of Himself so we can receive eternal life (*The Holy Bible, New International Version,* 2011/1973, John 3:16-17). Knowing all this, we can safely deduce the characteristics of Jesus as the Good Shepherd.

The Good Shepherd Lays Down His Life for Us

Jesus chooses to do the hard thing; He sacrifices for us. That's what makes Him the Good Shepherd. Any other shepherd might feel reluctant to lay down his life, but the Good Shepherd does it.

Recognizing the significance of Jesus' sacrifice on the cross will help us understand His goodness. His journey to bring us salvation wasn't easy. It was filled with struggle and resistance along the way, but Jesus endured because His love for us was too great. He endured being rejected by the very people He sought to rescue, being stoned, tortured, and ultimately bleeding out on the cross for us.

In His Good Shepherding, Jesus paid for our sins with His life. Not because we asked or even welcomed the weight of His sacrifice, but because He is good. His nature is unchanging.

John 10:11 says that the Good Shepherd lays down His life for us. God demonstrates His love for humanity by fulfilling His plan of redemption through the blood of the cross. His death and resurrection became a symbol of love in action—a love that not only declares affection but also walks it out and lays down its life as evidence.

The Good Shepherd constantly intercedes for us. He steps in to transform eternal suffering, which is the consequence of sin, into eternal life in Him. Jesus laid down His life so we can know God is for us and will never leave or forsake us. Jesus rescued us by laying down His life, and this is proof that He can be trusted. The Good Shepherd is faithful, and He loves us all personally.

It's such an honor to know that we are held in His very capable hands.

The Good Shepherd Provides for Us

Jesus' death and resurrection mean that we could have unlimited connection to our Heavenly Father. The Good Shepherd provides for His sheep, even by sacrificing Himself. Jesus loves us so much that He is willing to give us everything—His own life—in accordance with God's will.

Not only does Jesus provide our salvation, but He also provides what we need to thrive here on Earth. Because of Jesus, the Holy Spirit lives in us as the provider of our strength, direction, comfort, help, and so much more. We don't need to look too far for wisdom and guidance because the Good Shepherd is with us—ready to provide what we need.

The world may try to convince us that other providers are outside of Jesus, but the truth is in His Word. No degree, qualification, status, money, possessions, or worldly power can give as God provides. Nothing outside of Christ's provision can satisfy us; only He can.

Sometimes, we fall into the trap of believing the lies of the world. But the good news is God doesn't withhold His provision. Even when we fall prey to the deception and lies of the world and seek provision outside of Him, He embraces us as soon as we run back to Him after the world disappoints us. God is true to Himself.

Our actions don't stop Jesus from being the Good Shepherd who doesn't hold back from giving us what we need. Because His provision is complete, we can say, "The Lord is my shepherd, I lack nothing" (***The Holy Bible, New International Version,* 2011/1973, Psalm 23:1**). Jesus wants to provide nourishment for His sheep.

The Psalm of David clearly portrays the Good Shepherd as a faithful provider whose cup for us overflows and who anoints us with oil. Biblically, anointing a guest with oil symbolized the host's goodness and generosity. Jesus does that for us. He doesn't give anything in halves because He is an abundant shepherd. Jesus' goodness is demonstrated in that He gives generously to His sheep—all we need to do is walk with Him and ask for what we need.

The book of Luke is clear that when we seek God, we will find Him, and when we ask of Him, He will freely give to us (***The Holy Bible, New International Version,* 2011/1973, Luke 11**:9).

While other shepherds may withhold love, gifts, nourishment, and all sorts of good things, the ultimate Shepherd does not. Jesus is good because He only ever withholds with our best interests and needs in mind. He wants to give us safety, rest, and comfort, providing for us in every aspect. So take your concerns to Him and allow Him to reveal Himself as Jehovah Jireh, the Lord who provides in your life (**Motl, 2024**).

The best part of the Good Shepherd's provision is that it is both daily and eternal. God provides for our smaller, seemingly mundane needs because He cares. Consider Abraham and Isaac in Genesis 22. Abraham trusted that the Lord meant what He said and would provide for him according to His promises.

Even when faced with the test of sacrificing his son Isaac at the Lord's request, Abraham complied. If it wasn't for the angel who stopped Abraham at the altar, his son would have been an offering to God. Abraham's willingness to obey led him to become the father of nations. He trusted God's timing and lived with a mindset centered on the Lord as his provider—and God rewarded him.

It turns out that God also had a plan for Isaac. He made him the husband of Rebekah, and they became a significant part of Christ's lineage. Not only did God provide in the moment, but He also kept true to the future plans He had for Abraham and Isaac.

Throughout the Bible, particularly in the Old Testament, we see a continuous foreshadowing of Jesus' mission. God not only provides for people like Abraham in the day-to-day but also for us with eternity in mind. Jesus became our ultimate provision so that we may not only be saved today but also "have eternal life" (***The Holy Bible, New International Version,* 2011/1973, John** 3:16). God's regard for us is amazing because He considers it all.

God has not forgotten you, either. Whether you know Him or are still figuring out your faith, He has a plan for you! He sees your need and is eager to be Jehovah Jireh in your life. God wants to reveal Himself as the Good Shepherd who attends to your financial needs, cares for your relationship struggles, restores your health, gifts you with wisdom, and so much more.

We may not always see the bigger picture of the Good Shepherd's provision, but that's okay, because *He does.*

The Good Shepherd Guides Us

God guides us, and it is a great comfort to know that our direction comes from the Good Shepherd who holds the future and sees it all. He knows what traps are ahead of us and what we need to avoid them.

The Holy Spirit will prompt us when He wants to direct us to safety. With so many uncertainties in life, the journey can feel uncomfortable. But Jesus stands beside us as our guide through it all. He is there with us, helping us through the confusion, fear, financial overwhelm, sadness, and every other challenge that comes with life.

Some experiences that people face, such as job loss, broken relationships, financial setbacks, declining health, and other major obstacles, can cause them to forget the Good Shepherd's nature. We need the Good Shepherd to guide us through these valleys—and He does. It's up to us if we choose to follow Him.

Jesus shepherds us without force. "He guides me along the right paths for his name's sake" (***The Holy Bible, New International Version, 2011/1973*, Psalm 23**:3). His guidance is gentle and intentional. Jesus shows us a better way to live by calling us to Himself. After all, He is the way to Heaven, the truth, and the life (**refer to John** 14:6), and it is only in Christ that we are strengthened to live by faith and not by sight.

Because God is the Good Shepherd, He goes before us in everything. He will not let us go where He doesn't provide. Even when we go through trials and our lives feel like they are at the lowest of lows, Jesus is right there with us. He is committed to guiding us, one by one, to safety.

It is sweet to receive guidance from the One who truly knows the way. In **John 10:9,** Jesus reveals that He is the gate through which we enter to be rescued from the wilderness and brought into greener pastures. Whenever we are in Christ, we enter into an abundant life. We are blessed with direction, knowing where He wants us to be at all times. The Good Shepherd guides us through Scripture, fellowship, acknowledging His will, and living by faith.

The Good Shepherd Unites Us

Jesus is the plan of salvation that God sent from Heaven so that we can become part of the body of Christ. God came to offer Himself in place of our trespasses. When we turn to Christ, we receive the greatest gift we could ever imagine: to be filled with the Holy Spirit. When we gather as His sheep in the pen, He guides us, unifying us by the power of God within us as His church.

While bad or false shepherds come to cause chaos and division, Jesus (the true Good Shepherd) comes to bring harmony and unity. The Good Shepherd came so we "may have life, and have it to the full" (*The Holy Bible, New International Version,* **2011/1973, John 10:10**).

Jesus desires to unify all of God's sheep so Heaven can be filled with His greatest creation. It hurts God to lose even one, so He willingly leaves the 99 sheep to find the one who is lost. Even when we are outside the pen, roaming and lost, the Good Shepherd pursues us because He loves us. Every single sheep is priceless to Him.

The Good Shepherd Loves Us

The reason God gave Himself for us is the love He has for His people—the sheep of His pasture. The language of Jesus' ministry on earth and His death and resurrection is love. None of it would have happened if it weren't for His desire to be in a loving relationship with us. Love is the motive behind everything God does, and that's what makes Him the Good Shepherd.

The Good Shepherd always acts in a way that communicates the depths of His love for us. Sometimes, we need to remember the weight and glory of the beautiful truth that Jesus loves us. Jesus' love even comforts us in the valley of our lives. When we are going through tough times and fighting the battle against anxiety, the Good Shepherd stays with us and comforts us through it.

Jesus' love is unfathomable and remarkable. In **John 10:11–21**, we see four ways the Good Shepherd demonstrates His love. First, we see that the Good Shepherd's love is sacrificial, as He gave Himself as payment for our sins so that we could receive salvation through Him. Then, we see that Jesus' love for us is intimate. He longs for closeness with us and doesn't leave any of us behind.

In the same chapter, we see that the third aspect of Jesus' love is inclusivity. The Good Shepherd's heart is for us all to be with Him. He seeks to save both the believer and nonbeliever because He loves and desires us all. Because of His great love, Jesus invites us all to be safe with him. He sends out an individual call for each person to follow Him. The fourth aspect of His love is that it's voluntary. Jesus' love is not based on our works, thoughts, behaviors, or deeds; it is purely a result of who God is.

Keith Evans puts it well **(2023)**:

> If ever there is a question about whether God loves us, the biblical solution is not to look to ourselves, our love, or our faithfulness. Instead, we are called to look at the objective reality of what God has done for us in Christ. We are to ground our certainty and assurance of His love in who He is and what He has done—not in ourselves, which is ever-shifting sand. (para. 9)

Jesus' love is a sure foundation. It's not like human love that changes with the seasons, losing interest over time. We are so blessed to have a Good Shepherd who knows and loves us beyond what we could ever comprehend. We can trust and rest in His love.

He is the great I Am, the Alpha and the Omega. No one goes to Heaven except through Him. Also, God's love is personal. It's for each person, whether you know Him or are still working your way toward that closeness—He chooses you. When last did you stop to think about the depths of His love?

The Good Shepherd Knows Us

That's right! Jesus lays down His life for us, *knowing* that we are prone to making mistakes and entertaining sin. He chooses to love us, fully aware of our humanity and the frailty that comes with it. After all, He is God. Much like how an engineer knows the inner workings of their creation, God knows our inner workings. You would think He'd pull away and choose perfection instead of us, but He remains faithful to leading and loving us. God is a Good Shepherd because He wants the best for us, even knowing everything about us.

Before the Good Shepherd, we were living in our sheep-like behaviors—utterly hopeless. But He came and pulled us out. Jesus drew from His intricate knowledge of us to reveal Himself in the way we needed most. Because He knows us, He knew that there was nothing we could do to secure our eternal place with Him.

By giving Himself, He created a way for us to know and be with Him. He did this so we could access His provision, love, and safety. God saw all the sinful struggles we battled with beforehand and still adopted us into His family.

The Good Shepherd Keeps Us Safe

Jesus cares for His sheep and wants to keep us safe. He expresses care by laying down His life for us. If we look at **John 10:11–12**, Jesus speaks about how, as the Good Shepherd, He lays down His life for His sheep. Yet, someone who does not own the sheep doesn't put any care into keeping the flock safe. Even shepherds who have sheep neglect the flock to save themselves. But Jesus doesn't need saving from anyone or anything—He is the Savior. When we place our hope in everything else but Jesus, we risk being left vulnerable to the wolves when attacks come. We also risk being scattered.

However, **in John 10:14**, Jesus clearly states that He knows His sheep and would do anything to keep us safe, even sacrificing His life for us. The Good Shepherd is good because He gives up His life to provide His sheep a safe way home. He prefers to meet with danger and eliminate it rather than let us walk into the state of destruction.

Our salvation is not in our hands but in Jesus' very capable hands that were pierced for each of us. We'll only take instruction from a familiar voice that we trust, so it's important for us to get to know Jesus and the safety He provides more deeply.

It's expected that Jesus' sheep know the Good Shepherd's voice so we can respond when He calls us away from danger. Regardless, Jesus goes before us to keep us safe as the Good Shepherd. He clears the path, finds water, leads us to green pasture, and prepares our provision. The Good Shepherd guides us out of danger and bondage into stillness and victory.

His love for us compels Him to put Himself in the line of fire to keep us safe. While a bad shepherd would abandon the flock, the Good Shepherd prioritizes us. Jesus is committed to our safety from when we wake up in the morning to when we go to sleep at night. He is always eager to lead us. All we need to do is follow Him.

Chapter 2:

The Sheep's Posture

People can become downcast and discouraged, putting themselves in positions of panic and anxiety. I don't know if you've seen a sheep when it's despondent, but it looks like it has given up on life. Its posture shifts entirely, and it falls onto its back—feet dangling up in the sky (**Harrison, 2016**).

Seriously, a sheep will lie there on the ground, looking hopeless, allowing gravity to take over. If left in this state, it can pass away in a matter of hours. That's how we behave when we live outside of the Good Shepherd's plan for us. Our posture becomes one of perpetual sadness and discouragement, to the point where we need the Good Shepherd to intervene and rescue us.

We are completely dependent on the Good Shepherd to help us, and we are in good hands when we choose to follow Him. Sometimes, we get caught up in the things of this world that cause us to stray, sleep, run, and fall. Yet, Jesus loves us and cares for our well-being, always finding and helping us. The sheep's posture is of complete reliance. Our journey is to recognize that the only true help we can ever receive is in God's love, guidance, and presence.

Sheep tend to wander and move away from what the shepherd instructs them to do. Consequently, they must be continuously brought back to their original place, which is where the Good Shepherd comes in. Sheep need the Good Shepherd to restore them—to bring them back to their original place. Similarly, we are prone to hazardous behaviors. We act in ways that subject us to danger and hurt. But the Good Shepherd sees our harmful patterns and restores us.

Because of our damaging behaviors and decisions, the Good Shepherd watches over us closely. He is there whenever we fall or become despondent in life. He lifts us and puts us back in a healthy position.

The Good Shepherd is faithful in meeting all His sheep's needs, and we should remain focused on Him. While our behaviors are predictable to God, He still makes provisions for us when we fall short.

Sheep Behaviors

The natural behavior of sheep is to be unbothered. They feed, socialize, move, sleep, and run. Anyone who is a farmer or owns sheep knows how to provide good grazing land for them to eat every day. Jesus, as our Good Shepherd, is no different. He understands our daily needs and ensures they are taken care of within the pen.

Also, sheep instinctively walk in groups (flocks) because unity provides them with safety. When one sheep separates from another, the remaining flock becomes destabilized and lives in fear (**Goodling**, 2018). Real-life sheep are aware that they need each other for safety and to thrive.

If you drive past the countryside, you'll rarely see a sheep grazing or sleeping alone. That's because being together in the field comes naturally to them. Even when sheep are separated from their families, the bond between them is so strong that the family will remember the sheep when it returns (**Goodling**, 2018).

We are called to have the same heart toward our fellow brothers and sisters. When someone returns to the pen, no matter how long they've been away, it is our responsibility as the flock to be glad they are home.

Also, sheep move, but not just anyhow or anywhere. Sheep typically follow a leader from one destination to another. Farmers will tell you that if you can get one sheep to follow in one direction, the rest are likely to get up and join in (**Goodling**, 2018). Our relationship with God is no different.

He is our leader, the Good Shepherd, and the only direction we should move in is the one He takes us.

Sheep Characteristics

As you may know, sheep often need rescuing because they don't make the best decisions. We can also do pretty unnecessary and reckless things. Like real-life sheep, people can be stubborn, docile, timid, and defenseless (**Goodling**, 2018). We can mindlessly walk a path without in-depth knowledge of where it's taking us. Though we normally stick with our people (the flock), we can wander outside the parameters set for us. Therefore, it's easy for us to end up asleep, lost, or having fallen into a pit.

God likens us to sheep because a lot of our characteristics and behaviors are similar to those of sheep in the pasture. Fortunately, we have a Good Shepherd who understands us deeply enough to help us along the way.

The other fascinating thing about real-life sheep is that they only follow a leader they know and trust. You can't put a stranger in front of a flock and expect them to fall in line. If anything, they are more likely to treat a stranger like darkness—something frightening they need to run from. To build rapport with sheep, it's always good to approach them with gentleness and slowly. Any Good Shepherd knows this. Jesus is intentional and gentle with each of us because He knows our behaviors.

Of course, the topic has nothing to do with real animal sheep but everything to do with us—believers and those who are still seeking. We draw parallels between us and sheep because their behaviors are very similar to ours as people.

I mean, think about an average day. We wake up, eat, wash, work, exercise, and sleep. It may not be all these things or in this order, but that's all we do on a typical day. Because of our natural behavior, we can find ourselves not making time for God and the things of His kingdom. Some might say we live as sheep on the run or in hiding. We need Jesus as a provider for our needs, as our dominant leader, to guide us in the right direction. We also need Him to protect us when we sleep and to bring us back home when we are lost, stray, or run away.

Jesus doesn't hold sheep-like behaviors against us. Instead, He calls us to surrender to Him so He can use these behaviors for His glory. The Good Shepherd takes the load off us as we are pulled to focus on Him. We are the sheep of His pasture, and He'll never stop putting Himself on the line for us. After all, He welcomes us home with open arms as the father does with his prodigal son. We'll explore more about the prodigal son parable in Chapter 4 when we uncover how Jesus' sheep can stray.

The motivation behind writing about sheep comes from the realizations I've had as a pastor for over seven years. I've watched people do things that blow my mind. In the beginning, I thought that God's Word would just change people. However, I soon realized that people have behaviors that sometimes cause them to pull away from the transformation that God desires for them. Yes, the Word of God is powerful, but it cannot be active in your life if you do not know the Good Shepherd—Jesus.

People of God: The Sheep of His Pasture

Biblically, people raised sheep for nourishment through their wool, meat, and milk (**Swartzentruber**, 2011). Not a single part of the sheep was wasted; even their skins were used to make writing parchment. Before Jesus gave His life for our eternity, sheep were so essential to the faith walk that they were also used as sacrifices so people might remember the coming of Jesus.

Even in the ancient days of the Old Testament, sheep were always shown to struggle with taking care of themselves. They always depended on their shepherd to do that for them. The people of God are no different. Apart from Him, we are wasting away in attempts to survive and care for ourselves. But with Him, we are deeply cared for.

The Good Shepherd's primary responsibility is to love, provide for, and protect the sheep of His pasture, while the sheep's only job is to receive Him. We should embrace God's love and listen to His voice. We are people of God, and He wants us to dwell in green pastures so we can be nourished and enriched. As timid as sheep are, God's power at work within us gives us strength. Being in His presence keeps us safe. It's dangerous for us to lack protection from predators, but Jesus offers Himself as a hiding place for us. This is why we must shield ourselves in Him.

The Bible shows how important God's people are to Him. Consider the example of the Israelites, also known as the chosen people. God appointed Moses as a trustworthy leader to take them to the promised land. Once Moses' time was up, Joshua took up that position.

The point is that God is always eager to fulfill His promise of leading us. He loves us too much to leave us without guidance or help. Not only does He send people like Moses and Joshua, but He also offers the ultimate sacrifice for us—Himself. Jesus calls us near because He knows that He is the only one with the resources to keep us safe and prepare us for eternity with Him.

Jesus' sheep matter to Him, but we aren't always good at caring for ourselves. That's why the Bible frequently draws comparisons between us and sheep: We are not always the best at making good choices or caring for ourselves. Jesus is the Good Shepherd because He knows how to keep us healthy and safe. So we need Him to maintain His role as the Good Shepherd in our lives.

When we recognize our need for Jesus, we give God's Word the freedom to work in us and shape our lives. This requires us to take up a posture of surrender to His authority and let Him work as the ultimate leader in our lives. When we adhere to God's Word and hear His voice, we are kept in the security of His Good Shepherdhood.

We are instructed to know that the Lord is God. We ought to acknowledge that God made us, and we are the sheep of His pasture (***The Holy Bible, New International Version,*** **2011/1973, Psalm 100:3**). The pasture is a peaceful place where sheep go to eat. As Psalm 23 indicates, we are fed from *green pastures* because pastures that are overgrazed are no longer useful to the sheep. The greenery the Bible refers to symbolizes the abundance we receive when we surrender to God, finding food to eat in His pastures.

Recognizing that we are the sheep of God's pastures is an acknowledgment of trust. It declares that we trust the Good Shepherd's leadership and are willing to follow Him obediently. By nature, sheep are followers and must trust their shepherd. Similarly, when we trust Jesus, we call on His name in times of trouble. We also call on Him when things are going well, and we are up on our feet. Trusting in Jesus allows us to maintain a posture of confidence. We can stand firmly in faith, knowing that our help comes from a faithful Good Shepherd.

If it feels like life is just happening to you right now, and you are the despondent sheep lying on your back, be encouraged—you have a Good Shepherd who deeply cares for you. He won't leave you where you are; He is faithful in helping you change your posture. Jesus offers grace. Even if you are in a position that you created with bad choices and following the wrong crowd, He is faithful in helping you get back on your feet. So, never think it's too late to change your posture and face Him daily. You can always call on Jesus and trust in Him.

The Good Shepherd restores and brings us back to Him. God created us for Himself, so He would never leave His creation without help. The Holy Spirit within us is exactly that—our counselor, helper, and advocate in difficulties. God helps us get back on our feet and move forward for the glory of His name. At times, we may feel lightheaded, turned around, confused, or weak in the knees, but Jesus is by our side with every step we take.

By surrendering ourselves and our plans to God's will, we can see goodness emerge from even a difficult situation. All we need to do is consistently return to Him. If we are despondent and lying on our backs, we can call out to Him for help. Looking beyond our posture and reaching out to God for help gives us a better perspective in life, allowing us to notice the beauty and security in being completely reliant on Jesus.

The Good Shepherd offers us access to His green pastures, where we can be encouraged, find peace, and move in abundance. It's never too late to choose to follow Him wherever He leads. In fact, the first instinct of sheep is to follow, and we'll explore that in the next chapter.

Chapter 3:

Jesus' Sheep—Follow

How closely we follow the Good Shepherd is reflected in how well we know His voice. Unlike Instagram, where followers are surface-level, Jesus' sheep follow to establish a deep connection with God. Following Him is not about the perks, but about cultivating an honest, loving relationship with our Creator.

To follow Jesus means to commit our lives to Him, and this is the most liberating thing we could ever do. Committing our lives to Jesus can feel unsettling in the beginning. For instance, for those who are still searching for intimacy with Him, building that relationship can first feel like swimming in the deep end without a floaty—scary and uncomfortable. We might not know where to start or how to maintain momentum once on the journey of following Him. But take heart: Like every relationship, getting through the awkwardness and building a lasting connection takes communication, quality time, and patience.

Also, following the Good Shepherd involves being okay with missing out on world things. God stands above the pleasures and temptations of this world. Your entire life becomes about living a holy, set-apart life—one that's different from your peers or what the world finds attractive. That's not to say following Jesus can't be fun. Instead, following Him means dedicating each moment of your life to His will.

There's nothing more comforting and reassuring than giving full control over your decisions, thoughts, feelings, behaviors, words, beliefs, and anything else you can think of to the Good Shepherd. It's reassuring to know that God maintains His rightful place of authority in our lives because He can do no wrong. He makes no mistakes, which means everything that happens in our lives occurs with His backing. We can rest assured that His intention is to give us abundant, fulfilling, and hope-filled lives, all of which we cannot give ourselves.

Have you ever met someone who seems to have it all together? They are financially wealthy, their debt is paid off, they have no fears about money, and they can buy whatever they want, whenever they want.

Still, you see that same person unhappy and think, *But they have it all together. Shouldn't they be happy?* Many people who prioritize the world over God are standing on shaky ground. They can easily become like despondent sheep that have green pastures and everything provided for them, but without the Good Shepherd by their side, they slowly move toward spiritual death. This happens because material happiness can never replace the joy that comes from a life rooted in God. What Jesus gives to us when we follow Him is more valuable than gold.

Why Follow the Good Shepherd?

God is worth following because He revealed Himself as Father in creation, Jesus the Son in redemption, and the Holy Spirit in regeneration. Jesus' resurrection compels all who know of Him to trust in His faithfulness. He is God, worthy of our adoration, worship, love, and obedience. When Jesus' sheep follow Him, He pours abundantly into us, giving more than we could ever expect or hope for. He is the Good Shepherd because He does exceedingly more for us than we could ever repay or do for ourselves.

Jesus distinguishes Himself as the *Good Shepherd*, meaning there will be those who try to imitate His shepherding, but their efforts will fail. In **Matthew 7:15**, we are warned to watch out for false prophets who come as wolves in sheep's clothing—we can only do that when we follow the Good Shepherd.

This following is an act of submission to Christ's protection, preventing us from falling prey to the wolves of the world. When we get close enough to God, we are able to discern the Good Shepherd from the wolf in sheep's clothing who lurks outside of Christ. We follow the Good Shepherd for many reasons, and in doing so, we stand to gain so much more than He does by leading us.

Because He Leads

Leadership is at the heart of any success or downfall in life. We are led by our beliefs, where we put our trust, and so forth. What we allow to lead us determines where we end up. Suppose a group of friends are on a road trip, following one another toward the destination—one car behind another.

Suddenly, one friend decides they can guess their way to the destination, so they proceed to switch off the GPS. If this car gets lost along the way, the whole convoy is out of luck. They could get stuck in unfamiliar, dangerous areas. What was meant to be a fun trip with friends can quickly become scary and frustrating. Similarly, who we choose to follow will determine whether we end up at the right destination.

Thankfully, Jesus is a leader we can trust. He is all-knowing and has walked the road before us. The Good Shepherd is worth following because we are in capable hands when led by Him. He will always go ahead of us, guiding us along straight paths. Anything threatening to touch us cannot have access without passing through Him first. As Jesus leads us, He feels all we go through way before we experience it.

Because Jesus leads us, we are more than conquerors. Consider John 16:33, where Jesus says, "I have overcome the world," assuring us that nothing can harm us. Even when there are troubles coming our way, we are victors in Jesus (***The Holy Bible, New International Version, 2011/1973, John 16:33***).

Since Jesus goes ahead of us, it's important to know His voice. It is written in the Bible that Jesus' sheep follow Him "because they know His voice" (***The Holy Bible, New International Version, 2011/1973, John 10:***4). So we can't follow the Good Shepherd if He is a stranger to us. Think about it: You wouldn't randomly get into a car with someone you don't know. In the same way, following Jesus requires knowledge of Him. And it shouldn't be just theological knowledge, which is great, but more so an intimate connection and desire to be with Him.

Because He Saves

Nowadays, when we talk about saving, we only think of the monetary method. We save money for future children, plans, and so on. This is great and all, but it's not the saving I'm referring to here. I'm talking about how the Good Shepherd saves our souls when we follow Him.

He brings us out of darkness into life in Him (***The Holy Bible, New International Version,* 2011/1973, Colossians** 1:18). When He saves us, we experience redemption and forgiveness for our sins.

A benefit of knowing Jesus' voice through intimate connection with Him is we "will be saved" (***The Holy Bible, New International Version,* 2011/1973, John 10:9**). Jesus saves. What we are talking about here is the remission of our souls from the consequences of sin. He pulls us back from the fire and gives us a chance to choose life in Him. When we follow the Good Shepherd, He keeps us safe in His presence by shielding us from the thieves and robbers of this world.

Let me bring you back to the image of the despondent sheep, hours away from passing. In that scenario, Jesus comes toward us and pulls us back onto our feet. He saves our lives because He is the Good Shepherd who intercedes for us when we are meant to pass away.

Sometimes, we put ourselves in situations that lead to death because of our own sins. Yet, instead of stepping back and letting us experience the punishment for our sinful choices, Jesus saves us. He pays the penalty because He knows we can't afford to.

Jesus is the gate, and we enter the pen (His safety) through Him. When we are saved, nothing can change the way the Good Shepherd rescues us. Jesus says we "will come in and go out, and find pasture" because His safety is a sure thing (***The Holy Bible, New International Version,* 2011/1973, John 10:9**). The pen is in Christ, while the other side of the fence is outside of Christ. But He keeps His eye on us wherever we are because He cares for His sheep. Jesus is both the gate and the Good Shepherd who goes searching for those who have yet to enter and who need to re-enter Him.

Because He Gives Abundant Life

As the Good Shepherd, Jesus came so that we could have an abundant life (**refer to John 10:10**). That's another benefit of following the Good Shepherd! We get to live in hope in this fallen world because we know that He promises us eternal fullness. He is the *Good* Shepherd because He lays down His life for our eternity by giving Himself for us (**refer to John 10:11**).

To the world, abundance means possession. It means you have all the cars, clothes, and luxury bags you need. But to God, abundance is eternal. It's not necessarily measured by what you possess, but by who you are and how you view what you have in your hands. Jesus gives us abundant life, joy, mercy, goodness, and supply. Don't take my word for it; you can read this for yourself in Isaiah 55:7, Psalm 31:19, Jonah 4:2, and 2 Peter 1:10–11. Jesus is abundant; everything we need flows in and through Him.

The Good Shepherd is not afraid of the threats against the lives of His flock and will not run away at the sight of danger. He says so Himself in **John 10:13–17**, which confirms how He is wholeheartedly always willing to lay His life down for us. No one and nothing is powerful enough to take life from God, so it is awe-inspiring that He continually chooses to give His life for us, only to take it up again. That's right. In situations where other shepherds would run, Jesus demonstrates His goodness by persistently deciding to guard us with His life—all on His "own accord" (***The Holy Bible, New International Version, 2011/1973, John 10:18***). This means that, with all the authority Jesus has as God, He *chooses* to sacrifice for us because His love is personal. Who wouldn't want to follow such a remarkable Shepherd?

Because He Cares

In case it hasn't sunk in yet, salvation and intimacy with the Good Shepherd are personal! Jesus is worth following because He cares for you, whether you are a believer or someone still wrestling with your belief. God takes care of us in ways we cannot even imagine. He cares about how He preserves our lives and gives us opportunity after opportunity to return to Him. Jesus cares for us by shielding us from the consequence of sin, which is death, and ushering us into eternal life with Him. His mercies, which are new every morning, are another example of His loving kindness and care toward us.

Jesus is the Good Shepherd, and He is worth following because, after declaring that He is who He is, He shows no favoritism. Jesus tells us that He is the Good Shepherd. He says that He knows His sheep, and His sheep know Him, so He lays down His life to bring us to the pen with Him (*The Holy Bible, New International Version,* 2011/1973, John 10:14–16). This shows that Jesus is aware of those who know Him and dwell within the pen, as well as those who are outside of it, and He is concerned for each of us.

The Good Shepherd sees us in our mess and calls us each by name. He is determined to bring us all into the pen so we can be safe from danger. So never think that your faith walk is "not mature" enough or that you "aren't ready" to be in His presence. Do not count yourself out because Jesus never does. Your mistakes and shortcomings don't disqualify you from His love. In fact, He wants you to closely relate with Him so you can experience all the good He has in store for your life.

Everyone's journey to follow the Good Shepherd is unique. Fortunately, God is so good that He made provisions for those differences. In John 10, He speaks to both the sheep who stick close to Him and know His voice, as well as those who wander and sometimes end up outside of the gate. He is a Good Shepherd, worthy of following, because He doesn't pit His sheep against one another or prioritize one over another. Jesus values us all equally.

Follow the Good Shepherd: It Is Not a Contest, but a Relationship

Our relationship with God needs to be about substance, not about how much theology we can pack into our vocabulary to appear a certain way. Looking like good Christians or just appearing *good* to others doesn't make us that way. We are only transformed and made better when we allow the Holy Spirit to work in us.

Follow God. Accepting salvation is not a contest or competition to see who looks the best to the world. Actually, God looks at the heart, so our salvation is about transforming how we think, what we believe, and the condition of our hearts. Jesus is more concerned about matters of the heart than He is about appearances. In **John 7:24**, Jesus cautions us and instructs us not to judge by appearances. People may look happy but be miserable inside. They can flaunt their relationship with God in public but lack true intimacy with Him in private.

Appearance says knowing God is a contest; it's about who can perform better. Yet, Jesus says knowing Him is a relationship. It's about establishing closeness and transparency while seeing the fruit of His love grow in our lives. In the Bible, the Lord speaks to Samuel and tells him not to think about appearances because some may seem connected, but they are actually distant. The Bible says that we look at the outward appearance, but Jesus is concerned with the heart (***The Holy Bible, New International Version,* 2011/1973, 1 Samuel 16:**7).

In our relationship with God, nothing shakes us. Jesus becomes our place of refuge and stability. The Lord is our cornerstone when we are in a relationship with him; nothing in the world matters because our gaze is fixed on His. We can only truly be safe when we are deeply connected to the Good Shepherd. Otherwise, we are vulnerable to the enemy's schemes if we are performing for people rather than actually being close to Jesus. So, we should be careful of having a surface-level connection with the Good Shepherd. We are blessed that we can build genuine relationships with Jesus, who saves, heals, provides, and, most of all, calls us His own.

We follow the Good Shepherd intimately when we share a genuine connection with Him. We know His voice and only receive counsel from Him, tuning out all others. There are many fake followers in the world; we see them on social media. We see many people claim to know one another and connect, but no one truly knows about the next person. Let's not fall into the trap of mimicking this behavior when approaching God. We have an opportunity to enjoy the connection with our Creator, so let's not squander it. When we follow the Good Shepherd, our knowledge of Him needs to be personal and deep. It is more fulfilling to know Jesus and lose the world than anything else.

When we are not close enough to God, we'll see it in our patterns. We may come in and out of the pen. For example, we may find ourselves going to that party we shouldn't attend, talking behind someone's back, living joyless lives when Jesus offers us joy, and so much more. It is only when we are in a relationship with the Good Shepherd that we are safe and satisfied.

A sense of grounding and trust happens when we genuinely follow the Good Shepherd. When we lean into God's love, we become trusting people who can follow Him no matter what. I will rejoice "no matter what," and I will overcome "no matter what." We ought to trust in God wholeheartedly and not lean on human understanding (***The Holy Bible, New International Version,* 2011/1973, Proverbs 3**:5–6). This is what a relationship with Jesus helps us do.

Our personal relationship with Jesus enables us to stay with Him even when circumstances are not favorable. It consoles us to remember that Jesus came to fulfill the law so we can have eternal access to Him. Knowing the Good Shepherd and having a genuine relationship with Him shifts our focus away from external situations and draws us toward deeper intimacy with Him.

Jesus' love for His flock turns religious customs into a genuine relationship with the Father. And life is just better with Him. When we enter the pen and are close to Jesus, it starts to change us. Inside the pen, we live in service to God and no longer engage in habitual or mechanical actions. Instead, we enjoy His love and feel His security. We'll never change if we don't get close to the Good Shepherd.

Think of the closeness between parents and children. I know my daughter listens to my correction and won't do something my voice guides her not to. She knows my voice and my wife's to the point where she's attentive to what we say. It's the same with us and God. When we know His voice, we follow Him without reservation. Knowing His voice also keeps us from falling prey to wolves in sheep's clothing.

Nowadays, people are indecisive about what God calls them to do. This means we quickly become susceptible to avoiding accountability. When we drift away or stray, which we will discuss in Chapter 4, we no longer feel His presence as deeply as closeness allows. Worldly pressures will crush us without the Good Shepherd. However, when we are close to Him, we can distinguish God's voice from the deception of false prophets.

It's a lot easier to serve and live by the fence of the pen than at the front, but the latter is essential. We need to let Jesus bring us closer to him. Having one foot in the pen and the other out puts us in danger. God wants us to get off the fence (***The Holy Bible, New International Version,* 2011/1973, Revelation 3:15-16**) and walk with Him, step by step. He wants us to get into the flock and be unshakeable and close. So draw nearer to Him. It's the best decision anyone can make for themselves.

How to Follow the Good Shepherd

The reality is that everyone can improve their relationship with God. An improved connection with God begins when we let His power lead and sustain us. Wanting to follow the Good Shepherd is a great spiritual goal for each of us, and we can all benefit from drawing near to Him daily.

Whether you are a believer or someone seeking Jesus, there are ways to follow Him. None of us are too far for God to reach or too distant to return to Him. We can ask God to give us a spirit that is willing to follow Him and sustain us in the joy of His salvation (***The Holy Bible, New International Version,* 2011/1973, Psalm 51:12**). We can choose to follow Him no matter what part of the world we are in, and He will sustain us in our walk.

If you have reached a point in your life where you want to be closer to God, you are not alone. Many of us want to follow Jesus but have no idea where to start and what it takes to remain in the pen with Him. At first, following the Good Shepherd can feel super challenging, especially when we try to do it with our own strength. But the Lord takes us through it all if we accept His invitation. To start your journey of following Jesus, you can pray the Psalm of David, written when he was in desperate need of God after committing adultery, "Create in me a pure heart, O God, and renew a steadfast spirit within me. Do not cast me from Your presence or take Your Holy Spirit from me" (*The Holy Bible, New International Version,* **2011/1973, Psalm 51:10–11**). Don't stop at this prayer; do things that bring you closer to God daily.

Thankfully, the Bible tells us how Jesus' sheep can follow the Good Shepherd. It presents ways to help us increase our faith and draw nearer to God. The move toward Jesus is a daily decision, and it starts with implementing changes today.

Believe in Jesus and Understand He Is God

Believing in Jesus requires us to rely completely on Him. We do this first by accepting Him as the Lord and Savior of our lives. It is written that if we declare that Jesus is Lord and believe this declaration with our hearts, we will be saved (*The Holy Bible, New International Version,* **2011/1973, Romans 10:9**). Our belief in Jesus begins with confession. Welcome Him into your mess and let God change you from the inside out.

Secondly, believing in Jesus requires us to put our hope in Him. After all, our faith needs to be in action as a demonstration of complete trust in God. As the Apostle Paul shares, "Now faith is confidence in what we hope for and assurance about what we do not see" (*The Holy Bible, New International Version,* **2011/1973, Hebrews 11:1**). Belief in Jesus and the understanding that He is God is rooted in a faith that recognizes His power. He is the God who created the entire universe by commanding the invisible to become visible.

Your faith will help you continue to follow the Good Shepherd in confession and action. Also, be faithful and walk through the gate that has been provided for you. It's not our works that sustain us in the pen, but His sacrifice and the faith He sees in us. Ephesians 2:8-9 says that it is by grace, through our faith, that we are saved. Our works and public appearances—though they matter because they are a representation of the changed heart posture—have nothing to do with it. So start following the Good Shepherd by believing that He is God.

Foster a Personal Relationship With Him

Fostering a relationship with Jesus builds trust so you can always cling to Him. Children who have learned to trust their parents typically believe their needs will be met. Similarly, when we know God through a personal relationship, trusting Him as our Good Shepherd and provider is easier. We will not worry about whether we'll be taken care of because our closeness to God will make it impossible to believe anything outside of the truth that He is Jehovah Jireh—the Lord who provides.

We foster a personal relationship with Jesus by honoring Him with everything we have—our time, efforts, belongings, bodies, finances, and so on. In honoring Him, we consciously remember that all we have, down to the very breath in our lungs, is impossible without Him. Also, honoring God with our time means being in the Bible, spending time in worship, and connecting with people who support and challenge our faith. We learn God's voice when we are close to Him, and knowing it helps us follow the Good Shepherd without reservation.

Know His Voice

God is always speaking and instructing us. To hear Him, we need to fine-tune our receptiveness to His voice. How? Well, we do that by reading the Bible. The voice of God is present throughout the Scriptures. When you read His Word, you learn His character, which helps you distinguish His instruction from other deceptive voices. No one can claim to know God without adhering to His Word.

Also, quiet time with the Lord is a great way to familiarize yourself with His voice. The more time you spend with your family, the more you understand who they are and their expectations.

Similarly, when you set aside time to be with God and just listen to what He has to say, the more you'll understand and draw near to Him. Moreover, knowing Jesus' voice is all about intentionality. We must intentionally spend time with Him, get closer to Him, seek Him, and ask Him questions about the things we don't understand. No one has ever regretted making room for God's glory in their lives—so go all in.

When you know God's voice, it's easier for you to follow Him. "When He has brought out all His own, He goes on ahead of them, and His sheep follow Him because they know His voice" (***The Holy Bible, New International Version,* 2011/1973, John 10:4).** The Scripture is clear: We follow Him *because* we know His voice. This allows us to notice and refuse anything that contradicts who the Good Shepherd is. What are you doing today to be attentive to the Good Shepherd's voice?

Stay in Church

Jesus said, "For where two or three gather in my name, there am I with them" (***The Holy Bible, New International Version,* 2011/1973, Matthew 18:20).** Church is a gathering of believers to praise, bless, and exalt the name of Jesus. A thought pops up in my mind about how people visit the doctor when they're sick; in the same way, we go to church. You see, the gathering of saints is not just for those who already know Jesus; it's actually for those who are searching, feeling lost, wandering, questioning, fearful, weary, afraid, or in desperate need of Jesus—all of us fit into at least one of these categories.

Staying in church opens the door to remarkable blessings. Remember, God uses the people around us to bless us. When you stay in a church community, you see Christ's body at work. The kindness, welcoming nature, grace, encouragement, correction, and support that come with being part of a church community are unmatched.

Of course, I'd like to say all churches are composed of people who represent Jesus well, but that's not always the case. Sometimes, the biggest disappointments come from churches, which is unfortunate. However, as people build their faith in Jesus, we must remember that these flaws aren't new to this generation of churches.

Old churches also had their share of problems because, just like sheep, people make mistakes! These issues are clear in Paul's letters to the different early churches.

Paul wrote a letter to the first church, the church in Ephesus, addressed to the Ephesians (***The Holy Bible, New International Version, 2011/1973, Revelation 2:1–7***). Jesus saw this church's hard work, strong doctrine, and firm determination and found them commendable. However, all these things had overshadowed the people's love for God. Many people fixate on doctrine without embracing God's love. Yes, gathering to correct and rebuke one another is good, but without God's love, the correction comes from a place of condemnation and doesn't lead to restoration or encouragement.

Paul also wrote letters to six other churches: the persecuted church of Smyrna (**see Revelation 2:8–11**), the compromised church in Pergamum (**see Revelation 2:12–17**), and the corrupted church in Thyatira (**see Revelation 2:18–29**). I could unpack each of these, but it would need another book.

Our duty is not to leave the church community because of its flaws, but to be a functional part of it. How? Well, by representing our Lord and Savior, Jesus Christ. We've got to remember that the church is important to Jesus. From Christ's point of view, the church is not a building but a gathering of people with hearts after God's. It's a place where we actively pursue Jesus together! In fact, the church is so important to Jesus that the Bible refers to it as His bride. If Jesus can see the imperfections in His bride and love her anyway, we should follow His direction. Prioritize gathering with others to exalt the mighty name of Jesus Christ. We should treat the church respectfully—show up on time, speak well of our fellow brothers and sisters, and go out into the world in service.

If you haven't yet accepted Jesus as your Lord and Savior, please seek an opportunity to do so. But also, don't let religious, persecuted, compromised, or corrupted churches keep you from knowing the Good Shepherd. Get to know Him for yourself. Seek Him, and keep seeking Him until He reveals a trusted community of people with whom you can gather in His name.

Just as sheep move together in a flock, it's essential for us to build community. We should move and do this walk together. Church is not a single-day engagement; it's a daily commitment to developing a connection with the Good Shepherd by following Him closely with the rest of His flock. It requires each person to join a community of people who will hold them accountable for the things of God's kingdom. Church is typically the best place to do that. A church community naturally builds us in faith, encourages us, and motivates us toward love and good deeds—refer to Hebrews 10:24–25.

Walk in Purpose

Keep moving in Jesus' direction—it's that simple. God prepared good works for us in advance, and we are God's handiwork (***The Holy Bible, New International Version,* 2011/1973, Ephesians 2:10**). We are made alive in Him, so we should use the gifts He has given us to glorify Him.

We cannot find purpose when we remove ourselves from the Creator of our purpose. God is life, so He is the essence of meaningfulness and the only one who gives purpose to all we do (**see John 14:6**). Outside of Him, there is no way, truth, or life.

Diligently Seek Him

"God did this so that they would seek him and perhaps reach out for him and find him, though he is not far from any one of us" (***The Holy Bible, New International Version,* 2011/1973, Acts 17:27**). The Good Shepherd wants us to seek Him, and He is neither far nor hiding. He is always right there, ready to lift us up if only we reach out to Him.

Diligently seeking God is about looking to Him for answers, assistance, guidance, fulfillment, and everything else we need. Instead of being so convinced that the world and its cultures can satisfy us, Jesus wants us to see that He is *the only satisfaction there is*. Unlike the things of this world that are temporary, God is eternal. Those who seek Him find Him and are satisfied beyond what they can imagine. Even David endorses in Psalm 14:2 that Jesus' heart for people is for us to seek Him. We should have hearts and visions fixated on who God is and what He desires for us. That's the true meaning of being His sheep and following Him.

Have a Heart of Gratitude

What can you thank God for today? It is a question that should be on our minds daily. Instead, we are stuck in competitive mode and comparison: *Oh, he has a bigger house than me. I wish our family was that close. The new iPhone would be so much better than the one I have.* Nowadays, many people are discontent because they compare themselves and their lives to others. Mind you, minimizing what we have and being discontent is a thief of joy.

We develop a grateful heart when we ask God to change our hearts and help us see what we can thank Him for daily. The Word of God instructs us to be joy-focused people, saying, "Rejoice in the Lord always. I will say it again: Rejoice!" (**The Holy Bible, New International Version, 2011/1973, Philippians** 4:4). Instead of complaining and comparing, let us focus our hearts on what we have.

For example, we have breath in our lungs, a roof over our heads, food to eat, at least one or two loving friends, hands to give, the mercies of God, which are new every morning, and so much more.

When we truly sit and reflect, we will realize that there's so much to be thankful for. Most of the things we take for granted are the very things someone out there is still praying for. Having a grateful heart is a solid way to follow the Good Shepherd, for sure.

Go Into the World and Share the Good News

We are encouraged to pursue discipleship by going out into the world and sharing the Gospel. Salvation isn't just for one or two people; it is for all. Jesus wants us all to be safe with Him in the pen, so we are on earth as testimonies of how good the "Good Shepherd" is! Once we experience His goodness, we should never keep it to ourselves.

"He said to them, "Go into all the world and preach the gospel to all creation" (*The Holy Bible, New International Version,* **2011/1973, Mark 16:**15). Jesus' example of ministry was proclaiming God to the people—**refer to Matthew 4:23**—and we should not hesitate to follow suit.

Stay Prayerful

Every relationship requires dialogue for communication to be effective, and prayer is how we communicate with God. He has given His Word so we can hear from Him; He also wants to hear from us, so praying is our response to what He has already said.

Developing a prayerful lifestyle immerses us in God's presence, allowing us to delight in the Good Shepherd. This closeness is guaranteed to bring more joy and peace into our lives. Then, we can live out Philippians 4:6–7, being anxious for nothing and making our requests known to God.

We don't always get it right when following Jesus. I've seen this in my own journey. Things can sometimes be all over the place. I realize I am like a sheep who has gone through many experiences—sometimes tired, other times motivated, and often a mix of both.

However, something must take root in us to become established in Christ. That way, the world and things outside the pen don't sway us. Jesus gives plenty of illustrations of what it means to follow the real thing versus the imitation. He is the real Good Shepherd, and when we stay in Him, no season or situation defines us but Him.

Be careful of becoming a sheep who follows by doing things that appear Christ-like but aren't rooted in Him. To follow Him, your faith walk needs to be less about appearances and more about closeness with God. Following Jesus is straightforward, but it's not always easy. Sometimes, we stray from His presence to do our own thing, only to realize that we are nothing without Him. Thankfully, the gate is always open, so we can return to Him. Next, we'll explore the reality of Jesus' sheep who stray—it's important because it can happen to any of us.

Chapter 4:

Jesus' Sheep—Stray

As Jesus' sheep, we follow, but sometimes, we drift away from the flock and attend to outside distractions. In search of something "better," we may stray from the pen, only to find that nothing of the sort exists because Jesus is remarkable, without comparison or rival.

Straying is a part of human behavior. It's simply what Jesus' sheep do. Sometimes, the reasons are conscious, while at other times, we stray because we become complacent and lukewarm in our faith. Some of us may not even notice that we've strayed until we are surrounded by people who are still in the pen, following the Good Shepherd closely.

With wayward priorities, straying almost becomes second nature. In **Matthew 6:33**, we are called to "seek first" the Kingdom of God and His righteousness because Jesus is fully aware that when our focus is elsewhere, our hearts and efforts will follow suit. Straying happens when we stop seeking or when God's kingdom is the last thing on our minds. It occurs when our focus, efforts, and hearts move away from God toward other, less worthy things.

Why Do We Stray?

To think we can keep ourselves safe or survive through our own deeds is foolish. God's creation cannot preserve itself. It's like saying sheep can provide, guide, and fight for themselves. We need the Good Shepherd.

We need Jesus to remain the savior, provider, and leader of our lives, or else we risk losing it all. We end up losing ourselves in this messy world. So, despite knowing all this, why do we stray? That's obvious:

We are the sheep of God's pasture. We were born with the instinct to sin, but Jesus came to pull us out of it. Just as people are born sinful from the time of conception (**see Psalm 51**:5), our default setting is to resist redemption and move toward sin. The good news is that God knows.

Sin

Bright, enticing, and shiny worldly temptations are everywhere, and we can easily fall into sinful patterns when we shift our focus away from the Good Shepherd. **Luke 15:11–16** paints a picture of a son who leaves his home with his full inheritance. After some time, he "squandered his wealth in wild living" (*The Holy Bible, New International Version,* **1979/2011, Luke 15:11–13)**. When we think of wild living, often something sinful comes to mind. In this parable, the son enjoyed temporary pleasures at the cost of his inheritance. He left home and made unwise choices.

The son must have thought the world outside the safety of his father's house had more and better to offer, only to find that all he truly needed was at home—where his father lived. The same is true for us sometimes. We stray from the pen, thinking there are better things other than following Jesus, only to learn that we can't live outside the pen without harm.

But there are other times when our reasons for straying aren't bright or enticing at all. Sometimes, we stray out of disobedience. We may convince ourselves to live sin-ridden lives by thinking our sin is "small" or "respectable" compared to someone else's. We can stray in sin, believing that we don't need a Good Shepherd to rescue us from anything. We convince ourselves that our sins are not as big or bad as others.

Yet, Jesus warns us about all sin. He says all of us are in need of His rescue because committing one sin is the same as committing them all (*The Holy Bible, New International Version,* **2011/1973, James 2:10**). So, no sin is better or smaller than another. Thankfully, God has compassion for us.

Even when we stray because of sin, He searches for us until He finds us. Jesus is the Good Shepherd because He has not left us sinful and without hope—we always have a path back to Him.

Feelings

Our sins are not the only things that cause us to stray; we also stray from believing our feelings. Shame, self-judgment, fear, pride, and so on are feelings that lead us away from the pen. But faith is not about feelings. It's about the truth. What God says about us and our situation is true, regardless of how we feel about it.

The Bible is clear that we must rely on and trust in God's plan alone. We can't live life guided by our feelings and expect to remain in the pen. It's usually our feelings that cause us to stray—chasing fame, wanting popularity, feeling hurt, or settling in disappointment. Feelings aren't truth; God is!

Our minds can produce certain feelings that may not align with what God wants for us. Proverbs 28:26 cautions us not to trust in ourselves because that's an act of foolishness (***The Holy Bible, New International Version, 2011/1973, Proverbs 28:26***). Instead, we are urged to walk in God's wisdom so we can be delivered from the spirit of doing what we feel.

We should go where Christ tells us to go, regardless of whether our minds support the instruction. To truly walk by faith and not by sight, as stated in **2 Corinthians 5:7**, we need to replace our feelings with God's Word. If we entertain what we feel and it happens to be a lie that's repeated long enough, we eventually accept it as truth—and there's a great danger in this.

Thankfully, we have the Bible to help us break the habit of believing our feelings. We can lean on God's Word so we don't lose sight of what's true and what He calls us to. When you feel tempted to do something that doesn't align with God's Word, stop in your tracks and pray. Hold His Word as a priority over what you feel. For instance, don't entertain sexual immorality, even when you feel like it, because your body is the temple of the Holy Spirit; honor God with it (***The***

Holy Bible, New International Version, 2011/1973, **1 Corinthians 6:19–20**). Following your feelings instead of the Good Shepherd can put you in spiritually damaging positions.

Fortunately, in moments of personal failure, much like the son who squandered his inheritance, we can quickly feel unworthy or unlovable, saying, "I am no longer worthy to be called your son; make me like one of your hired servants" (*The Holy Bible, New International Version,* 2011/1973, **Luke 15:19**). Yet, Jesus has already declared us chosen and loved (*The Holy Bible, New International Version,* 2011/1973, **Ephesians 1:4**–6). We have a stamp of eternal love on us, and our feelings can't change that. So when your feelings are trying to direct you, open the Word to search for what the truth says about your situation.

Not Knowing What We Seek

Sheep start to wander when they don't know what they are searching for. This wandering puts us in harm's way. Consider the prodigal son who wandered outside his father's gates, only to be met with the reality that the world would take all of his inheritance and leave him with nothing.

Sometimes, we don't know what we seek because we don't know the Bible. God's Word is all we need to know about Jesus, and that saves us from much wandering. For instance, the prodigal son wandered, not knowing the heart his father had toward him. So he left home thinking other people would probably be better than what's familiar. Yet, when he returned, he realized how deeply his father was fond of him all along, and his perspective shifted. We need to seek the Good Shepherd with intention and action; our faith can't stand alone. When we dive deep into who Jesus is, the spirit of not knowing what we seek is snuffed out.

Not knowing what we seek keeps us in a state of confusion and danger. If we are not focused on the Good Shepherd and seeking what He wants for us, we become distracted by unnecessary things that keep us from fulfilling our purpose in Christ. Often, not knowing what we seek is a sign that we've forgotten whom we belong to. We were created and redeemed by God. The Good Shepherd has compassion and mercy toward us, and we lose sight of Him when we stray. It's important to remember that the call and responsibility over our lives is to live in praise and worship of the Good Shepherd who laid it all down for us. When we know and remember who we are, we are more likely to seek Christ and His kingdom than to wander off, not knowing what we are searching for.

Finding Alternative Sources

Trusting God when the familiar is stripped away can be challenging. Sometimes, we feel more comfortable trusting Jesus if we have alternative sources or plans outside of Him. People like to feel in control of the next move, decision, chapter, and so on, but sometimes life presents us with entirely uncontrollable situations. That's when our faith is truly tested.

Relying on alternative sources to depend on looks like trusting that you are provided for because you have a stable job and income, without considering the possibility of it all being stripped away, leaving you feeling unfulfilled again.

Job is an example of how external sources can be stripped away. Though he was faithful and utterly dependent on God, Job's story reminds us of the risk we face if our hope is placed in alternative sources. For those who aren't familiar with Job's story, he was a devout worshipper and man of God. He was also quite rich in material wealth. Job had God, servants, property, financial freedom, and a beautiful family—he absolutely had everything he needed.

Suddenly came a time when his faith was tested. God pointed out Job's love for Him, noting it wasn't dependent on what he had, but on God's nature. Job's uprightness and decision to constantly turn away from evil delighted God (***The Holy Bible, New International Version, 2011/1973, Job 1***:8). Envious of this, the enemy proposed that Job's love for God was due to the blessings he had received from Him. The devil asked God to remove His hand and "strike everything" Job had, believing that Job's uprightness would end as soon as the blessings were stripped away (***The Holy Bible, New International Version,***

2011/1973, Job 1:**11). Disagreeing with the enemy's perspective, God gave the enemy permission to mess with every possession Job owned without causing any harm to the man himself (*The Holy Bible, International Version,* **2011/1973, Job** 1:12). So the purge of all that God had given Job began. But Job's uprightness and faith in God remained secure. Even after losing his home, wife, and children while battling health issues, Job declared the Lord faithful.

Of course, there were times when Job was frustrated because he didn't understand why God would allow things to keep falling apart in his life, especially when he had been a faithful servant of His. But even in that frustration, Job remained true to his trust in God.

He fell to the ground in worship, saying, "The Lord gave and the Lord has taken away; may the name of the Lord be praised" (*The Holy Bible, New International Version,* **2011/1973, Job 1:20–21**). The enemy's attempts to disrupt Job's faith did not succeed. As a reward for his steadfast faith, God blessed Job with twice what he had lost during the testing period (*The Holy Bible, International Version,* **2011/1973, Job 42:10).** But how often does the enemy get his way with us? How often do we miss out on God's abundance because we stop trusting Him?

When blessings are stripped away, how often do we question whether God is truly who He says He is and move on to find comfort in something else? Very few, if any, of us remain as steadfast in faith as Job did. When presented with the same trials, we are quick to seek alternative sources. We seek comfort in crystals, stars, moons, and signs—and are slow to see God's hand in the challenges. Yet, the Bible tells us to, "Be joyful in hope, patient in affliction, faithful in prayer" (*The Holy Bible, New International Version,* **Romans 12:12**). These are all things Job did, and the Lord didn't leave him in that place of lack for longer than needed.

We may want joy or peace in our lives and are misled into thinking we can find it outside Christ. Sometimes, we stray because we deceive ourselves into believing the hype that there's something better outside of the pen. We believe obedience to the Good Shepherd is for people who don't want fun or fulfilling lives. We stray because we want to find alternative sources, unaware we only need to be found in Jesus.

Alternative sources offer temporary satisfaction, unlike the Good Shepherd, who offers eternal fulfillment. You'll feel satisfied with sources outside the pen until you run out of whatever you draw from because everything outside of Jesus is temporary. That may be your bank account, social status, lifestyle, and maybe a person. When all that temporary stuff is stripped away, your only option is to depend on God. And sometimes, it's not until you hit rock bottom that you finally encounter the Rock of Ages—Jesus.

Returning to the Good Shepherd

Your returning to the Good Shepherd matters more to Him than the fact you've strayed. In fact, God even gives us His Word as a resource to help us return to Him. The Bible has endless revelations of who the Good Shepherd is, and sometimes we need those reminders to put us at ease as we plan to draw near. Jesus did not leave us helpless; He left us with hope in Him through the Holy Spirit. So, leaning into the Bible is essential for returning to the Good Shepherd. It is the switch that activates the Holy Spirit and the manual that guides us in the right way to go.

For those looking for redemption, Jesus is the redeemer. And for those looking to return to Him, remember He is the way and is always eager to have us back with Him. *But how?* This is a question you may be asking yourself, and this part of the chapter aims to explore what returning to the Good Shepherd looks like.

Choose to Return

Every big decision starts with a choice. You need to choose to return to Jesus for it to happen. I remember when life took a terrible turn for me at the age of 24. I watched my friends purchase homes and experience the reward of their discipline, while my own life seemed to be falling apart because of bad choices. So, I returned home to gain some perspective. I was brokenhearted. *How did I get here? What could I have done differently?* These questions were swarming around in my head.

One day, I went outside to sit on an old swing my parents had in the backyard, contemplating my purpose. My mom came out to comfort me. She didn't lecture or shout; instead, she extended compassion and embraced me as I laid my head on her lap. Imagine a grown man at 24, needing comfort from his mother. Well, I believe we are exactly like that with God. We are never too old to go to Him with our problems. We are never past the age of seeking comfort and returning to Him after straying. No confusion or contemplation gets in the way of God welcoming us back home if we choose to return to Him.

The best part is that God is always waiting to embrace and welcome us. Whatever your life's challenge may be, return to the Good Shepherd. Don't feel ashamed to find a swing in the backyard and lay your head on Him. He is good, and He cares for you. Also, His grace is sufficient, even in your iniquities.

This is demonstrated through the biblical parable of the prodigal son, found in Luke 15:14–18. The son in the parable returns home and is embraced, even after spending everything he has. He says, "I will set out and go back to my father" during his turning point (***The Holy Bible, New International Version,* 2011/1973, Luke 15:18**). Many of us need to realize that the point of return begins with this decision. No one can make it for us. The prodigal son could have let shame and fear keep him from going back home, but he didn't. Instead, he returned knowing that the consequences of straying would be kinder than the life he had been living away from home.

Certainly, to his surprise, his father welcomed him with open arms. Though the son had squandered his inheritance and feared his father would shun him, he was instead celebrated upon his return. If he hadn't made the decision to return, he wouldn't have experienced the joy of being welcomed back into his father's love.

Much like the prodigal son, you can make the life-changing decision to turn back to God at any point, as long as you have air to breathe in your lungs. In the story of the prodigal son, we are reminded that the father eagerly awaits our return. The same sentiment is shared in the parable of the lost sheep and the parable of the lost coin. Jesus *always* wants us to return to Him, no matter how badly we think we've messed up.

Choose to return. It doesn't matter how many times you miss the mark or make mistakes; the gate is always open for you. The Good Shepherd wants to celebrate your return to the pen. And as long as God's grace is with us, we can always return to Him.

The decision to return is the most challenging, yet the most fruitful thing you'll ever do. You can leave the enticing, sinful lifestyle behind (give it up) and return to the Good Shepherd's presence. Nothing outside the pen will fulfill you. We see this through the example of the prodigal son who left home. In fact, the world outside Christ is destructive and steals all that is rightfully ours in Christ. It steals the joy, the peace, and so much more. So let us learn from the prodigal son's story and choose to return to the safety and provision found in the presence of our Good Shepherd.

When you return to God, He places you right where He wants you to be. He opens His arms to you and celebrates your return, much like the father of the prodigal son. Straying from God doesn't make Him love you less; that's why He is happy to celebrate your return, just as the father did with his lost son. The parable is a perfect example of how Jesus welcomes us back into His presence when we decide to turn away from wild living and re-enter the pen. If we are wise enough to reject our pride, we can walk in the bigger purpose that God has for us. Pray that God lets you see beyond your selfishness so you can remain in and return to Him at all times.

Choose Repentance

Repentance is key to returning to the Good Shepherd. Our decision to turn represents a divine change of heart and steers us back to Jesus. Repentance can't happen if we think we are good and nothing is ever wrong. Instead, it begins when we recognize our weaknesses and take ownership of our mistakes. Poor decisions are a part of human nature, and God wants to work in our hearts to help us change the choices we make. But if we aren't honest with ourselves about our actions, it leaves little to no room for transformation to happen. Even in the parable, the lost son recognizes where he went wrong. When the son "came to his senses," it symbolized the shift, the turning that took place within him (***The Holy Bible, New International Version,* 1973/2011**, Luke

15:17). Similarly, our repentance begins internally. We must recognize when we've messed up and be able to admit it and then continue to submit ourselves to God, acknowledging our need for Him as the Savior and Creator of our lives.

However, it doesn't stop there. The prodigal son didn't stop at turning. Instead, he continued further into repentance. Upon returning home, the son told his father, "Father, I have sinned against heaven and against you. I am no longer worthy of being called your son" (*The Holy Bible, New International Version,* **1973/2011, Luke 15**:21). Once we've realized our mistakes and weaknesses, we should bring them to God—not in shame, but in transparency. Of course, God knows and sees all, even what happens outside of the pen. But our ability to be open and honest with Him, regardless of what He knows, is a true mark of a heart ready and willing to change.

The prodigal son acknowledged his sin and confessed it to his father, and that didn't change his father's love for him. The same is true for us. Instead of isolating us, repentance facilitates a foundation for reconciliation. With that said, recognition, confession, and reconciliation are all part of the process of repentance. Neither can happen without the other.

It doesn't change us to hide our sins or deny when we have strayed. However, confessing our shortcomings and allowing ourselves to receive God's love, even in accountability, changes the posture of our hearts. Indeed, we can learn a lot about returning to the Good Shepherd from the prodigal son.

Encounter the Good Shepherd in Low Moments

Straying can happen during our lowest moments. We might be seeking an immediate solution to a problem or an answer to things we have prayed for. During these low moments, we can easily be convinced that it's better to move away from Jesus in search of the satisfaction we seek. Yet, this is not true.

All the answers and solutions are found in the One who created life. They are all in God, so straying from Him takes us further from what we truly desire to know. Fortunately, the parable of the lost son shows how God embraces us at our lows. In the same way that the father prepared a feast for his son's return, Heaven celebrates every time our hearts return home. The question is: Are you willing to let God encounter you where you are?

Remember Where You Come From

You are a child of God, created in His image. This means you are chosen, loved, and a coheir through Christ. Even when you stray, remember that God longs to be with you in your low moments, so invite Him in. His grace is sufficient, as we are not worthy until we are transformed into His image through salvation. So, return to Him.

Encounter the Good Shepherd, who leaves the flock of 99 to find the one sheep that has strayed. God loves you. Love is His character, so nothing you do can change that.

It is written, "For I am convinced that neither death nor life, neither angels nor demons, neither the present nor the future, nor any powers, neither height nor depth nor anything else in all creation, will be able to separate us from the love of God that is in Christ Jesus our Lord" (***The Holy Bible, New International Version,* 2011/1973, Romans 8:38–39**). His love is as unchanging as His character. God is the same today as He was many years ago, and His love remains just as consistent. You need not be afraid when you rejoin the flock after straying because the Good Shepherd wants you near. Keep returning to Him, no matter how many times you stray.

Will you remember, at your lowest moment, where you came from? Your origin is in Jesus. He saved and redeemed you. Even when you feel worthless, recognize that the Good Shepherd calls you chosen. He is worthy, and He keeps you and adores you still. When we think we are self-sufficient, we forget that God bestows upon us life and worthiness. When we recognize our dependence on God's mercy, it becomes easier to celebrate when someone who has strayed returns to the flock.

Unlike the brother in the parable of the lost son, who compared and complained when his brother returned, we are called to celebrate each person's decision to return and stay close to God.

We ought to remember where we come from so we can constantly return to Him and celebrate those who join us in the pen. When we know who we are and where we come from, it leaves the enemy little to no opportunities to deceive us into straying again. The Bible tells us to "submit to God"—an act of remembering who we are in Him–and "resist the devil, and he will flee" (*The Holy Bible, New International Version,* 2011/1973, James 4:7). It's harder to resist the enemy's temptation and lies when we do not know the Good Shepherd or forget where we come from.

Jesus exemplified what this resistance looks like many times. For example, when the enemy tested Jesus in the wilderness, he didn't succeed because he knew where He came from. As God, Jesus responded to the enemy's tests with Scripture. He said, "It is written," before continuing to recite God's Word (*The Holy Bible, New International Version,* Matthew 4:4). So the same blueprint is true for us. When we get near to the Good Shepherd or turn to His Word during our low times, we are equipped to encounter Him and resist the enemy's schemes.

Identify and Address the Root of Straying

When you realize that you've strayed, be proactive in identifying the root of the problem. What enticed you? What's your sin? What did you long for when you felt you needed to stray from the flock to receive it? God's people should be solution-oriented. Your recognition of what went wrong can help you edify the communities around you as well. Your straying is not without purpose; it will all come together for God's glory.

If you aren't quite sure about the root of your straying, ask God to reveal it to you. He can show you what your heart's posture is so that you can recognize the root of some issues. Pray as David prayed, "Search me, God, and know my heart; test me and know my anxious thoughts.

See if there is any offensive way in me, and lead me in the way everlasting" (*The Holy Bible, New International Version,* **1973/2011, Psalm 139:23–24**).

When you can identify and address the root cause of straying, you can prevent making those same mistakes again. You also get the chance to witness firsthand how much you need God's help in your life.

Remember, His Presence Is Always With You

Sometimes, we believe God has forgotten about us when we stray, but that's far from true. Jesus is always with you. Even outside of the gate, He keeps His eyes set on you, seeing when and why you stray. He awaits your return in all seasons. Remember His presence and love in the tough moments so you can accept His invitation to guide and counsel you out of the darkness.

Even Psalm 23:4 reiterates this: "Even though I walk through the darkest valley, I will fear no evil, for you are with me; your rod and your staff, they comfort me" (*The Holy Bible, New International Version,* **1973/2011, Psalm 23:4**). The Good Shepherd doesn't leave us alone in the low moments. He doesn't deny us because we stray. Instead, He is with us, comforting and preparing a place for us.

When things are hard, or you are in a season of challenges, don't be afraid to call on Him. He is listening, and He will be there to comfort you. The biggest misconception is that you need to have things right and perfect before drawing near to the Good Shepherd. In reality, you can always come close to Jesus and let Him turn your mess into something beautiful. He isn't deterred or repelled by it. The Good Shepherd is with you at all times, and He chooses all of you.

Consider the Joy of Your Return

Just as the father in the parable of the lost son, Jesus responds with love when we choose to turn back from sin and return to Him. So our low moments don't change His love for us. In fact, He uses them for His glory and to show the world what He can do with messy situations.

Don't let your low moment be the reason you stop returning to Jesus. He is the Good Shepherd, so He is always ready to turn all ashes into something beautiful.

During your low moments, consider the joy of your return. Before the prodigal son could even get a word out, his father called on his servants to "bring the best robe and put it on him" (***The Holy Bible, New International Version,* 1973/2011, Luke 15:22**). The father instantly reverted to the position of being a good father who simply cared for his child despite his poor decisions. Hence, the father fed the prodigal son and had a celebratory feast for his return. The same is true for us with Jesus.

The Bible is clear that Heaven celebrates people who return to God. Our return doesn't go unnoticed or unappreciated—we are welcomed and embraced. Truly, that's how much the Good Shepherd loves us. He cares for us for His name's sake, despite our mistakes and the things we sometimes do to distance ourselves from His presence. Jesus claims us and calls us at all times because He is good. His love relentlessly pursues His flock.

What matters is not when you strayed or for how long, but your return to the arms of a loving father. The Good Shepherd sees us coming home while we are far from the gate, and He wells up with compassion. Just as the father with the prodigal son, Jesus springs to kiss us and throws His arms around us. Never allow your thoughts and shame to convince you that God prefers it if you stay away. He doesn't. He actually wants you to keep returning to Him until you stop straying.

You are never too much trouble for the Lord; His love and goodness extend further than any bad behavior on your end—so return. Come home to Him and consider the joy He will experience when you do.

In the parable of the prodigal son, the father never stopped loving his son or hoping for his return. No matter how far away he went from home, there was always a room in his father's house for him. Similarly, no matter how far we stray, there's room for repentance and reconciliation with Christ. Both the flock that remains in the pen and the stray sheep are His. Each is valuable to Jesus, and He wants us to be with Him.

He wants you safe and provided for. No amount of straying can change that. God wants you even as you wander outside His gates because *you are still His*. Without the Good Shepherd, there is a limit to your life and how much of your purpose you can fulfill. But with Him, there's no limit. You have boundaries as an ordinary person, but God works beyond those, so don't get comfortable operating without Him. Know that it is always the best decision to return to Him and let Him work all things together for your good. Your place is always there with Him, and He is ready to receive you. It's not too late for you to come home.

Many times straying is subconscious; it often happens when we don't devote ourselves to our relationship with God daily. However, people who don't stray could find themselves running from God, which is conscious behavior and will be discussed in Chapter 6. For now, let's look at what happens when we miss encounters in the presence of the Good Shepherd.

Chapter 5:

Jesus' Sheep—Sleep

While rest is essential, many of us end up sleeping through our days. The sleep we speak of here is not the physical rest we require but a lack of discernment. Our tendency to sleep through things that threaten to destroy us is why we need the Good Shepherd. He helps us stay awake in the most important moments.

Consider Jesus' journey in the garden of Gethsemane, which Matthew 26:36–46 focuses on. Jesus was with His disciples during the most sorrowful and troubled part of His life. He instructed them to sit while He went to a quiet area in the garden to pray. Jesus even shared with the disciples how His soul was overwhelmed with the reality of the coming crucifixion. He asked them to stay up "and keep watch" with Him (***The Holy Bible, New International Version,*** **2011/1973, Matthew 26:38**). At this point, Jesus was in agony, anticipating His impending death on the cross. He was deeply prayerful.

When He returned to His disciples after praying, He "found them sleeping" (***The Holy Bible, New International Version,*** **2011/1973, Matthew 26:**40). This is one of the hallmarks of our behaviors as Jesus' sheep: We sleep at pivotal moments in our faith and spirituality.

Jesus had instructed the disciples to keep watch, but when He returned, He found them sleeping. And that's how we can sometimes be in our own lives.

We either become so dependent on God's grace that we believe we can afford to doze off, or we become complacent and choose sleep over watchfulness. Yet, there's a reason Jesus instructs us to stay alert and keep watch. He already knows the danger that's coming. Jesus understands that we can't afford to be spiritually out of tune, lacking discernment, or asleep.

Because of His sovereignty and this being a matter of urgency, Jesus returns to the disciples and stresses His point by asking Peter: "Couldn't you men keep watch with me for one hour?" (***The Holy Bible, New International Version,* 2011/1973, Matthew 26:40**). I mean, seriously? That's how we are sometimes. We are given a task that the Good Shepherd knows we can do because He never gives us what we can't handle in His power. But we falter. We stray. We run. We sleep.

Again, Jesus instructed the disciples to watch and pray as He went to a quiet place for a second time. This time, He clarified the reason behind this request, saying, "Watch and pray so that you will not fall into temptation" (***The Holy Bible, New International Version,* 2011/1973, Matthew 26:41**). Even in His own agony, Jesus was looking out for His disciples.

He is the Good Shepherd who instructs us on what to do for our own good, not His. Jesus would still have had to die on the cross, regardless of whether the disciples obeyed Him. But because He was more concerned about His flock, He continued to guide them on how to avoid temptation.

An even better part of this is that the Good Shepherd wasn't oblivious to the disciples' weaknesses. Even as He instructed them to keep watch and pray, He knew that "The spirit is willing, but the flesh is weak" (***The Holy Bible, New International Version,* 2011/1973, Matthew 26:41**). He is aware that we will falter and probably give in to sleep. But He wants us to choose differently so we remain alert to what truly matters.

Jesus was trying to prepare His disciples for the trials ahead, but what did they do? They slept. He didn't want them to miss a thing. In the same way, He doesn't want us to miss a thing today, but we often do because we are Jesus' sheep. We take after the disciples' behavior and sleep when we are instructed otherwise. The theme of sleeping continued even after Jesus went away to pray for the third time, until Matthew 26:46, when the disciples were instructed to wake up and face Jesus' betrayer. How often do we, like the disciples, sleep through what God has instructed us to watch for?

When Sleep Endangers the Mission

Jesus' mission for the disciples was to sit, pray, watch, and be on guard, but they slept through it. The flesh overruled them, and they slept. They lacked discernment at a pivotal moment of their journey with Jesus in Gethsemane. Being spiritually awake and prayerful means we have a level of clarity and awareness about ourselves and the situation around us (**Kight, 2018**). On the other hand, a lack of discernment means we don't have situational or self-awareness, so we can only see as far as our eyes will let us—and that's not far when we're asleep.

Foolishness lies at the heart of poor discernment because spiritual sleep is usually marked by a high trust in self and a low dependency on God. The disciples received instruction from Jesus, yet instead of doing all they could to stay awake, they slept, leaving themselves vulnerable to temptation. Other causes of spiritual sleepiness include impulsive actions, conforming to worldly standards, and failing to exercise spiritual discipline.

Lack of discernment comes with a set of consequences. For example, falling into temptation, self-deception, situational blindness, recklessness, and failing to see what's going on within. The disciples fell asleep all three times after Jesus instructed them to watch and pray. Because of that, they couldn't prepare for Jesus' capture. When the hour came for Jesus to be handed over to His persecutors, all the disciples could do was to witness the betrayal.

Similarly, in our own lives, we sometimes create confusion and dismay because we sleep right through Jesus' guidance. So we enter certain seasons unprepared for what God has been preparing us for all along, and all we can do is to witness the trials. Much like the disciples, sleep makes us unprepared. As a result, we likely haven't prayed as we should when trials come or submitted ourselves to the Good Shepherd as instructed.

When we fall asleep during God's preparation, we lack the discernment and strength to stand up for what's right. Sometimes, we may not even understand why things are so challenging because we missed the memo about the entire trial beforehand. That affects our mission and our stance in Christ. We become susceptible to spiritual laziness and lack of purpose. However, Jesus doesn't leave us as we are—and that's the good news!

Even with all His efforts to prepare us and despite our lack of discernment, Jesus stays with us. He prays when we are asleep. He remains God and the Good Shepherd over our lives during our most vulnerable moments. We see this in how He didn't leave His disciples after giving them multiple chances of being watchful and prayerful with Him in Gethsemane.

Rather than sneaking away and leaving them alone to face the challenges they weren't prepared for, Jesus said, "Rise! Let us go! Here comes my betrayer!" (*The Holy Bible, New International Version,* **2011/1973, Matthew** 26:46). The Good Shepherd did not separate Himself from the sleeping disciples but continued to instruct them and remain with them during the time of trial.

Jesus calls us to wisdom—be awake. He wants to train us in the path we should take so that we are prepared for the trials we will face. But the enemy wants to tire us out. He wants us to take a nap at the wrong time and be caught off guard by trials and the difficulties coming our way.

When we don't know that an attack is brewing—maybe it's been building up for a while, and we didn't notice because we were sleeping—that's when we are most vulnerable to the enemy.

In **Matthew 26:36–46,** we see Jesus exemplify the type of preparation it takes to face intense trial, and He wants His disciples to stay up so they can learn from Him. The danger of sleeping at the wrong time is that we miss out on what God is showing us. In the text, Jesus displays sorrow, reverent prayer, and submission—qualities that those who follow Him should possess, but the disciples missed it all.

The enemy wants us to fall asleep in critical times when Jesus is trying to equip us with knowledge and guidance. The question is: Will we stay watchful and prayerful?

How to Remain Awake for the Mission

Life is complex, and many things can get in the way of our faith walk. Sometimes, these distractions keep us from hearing and doing what Jesus tells us. God's mission for us is clear and will always be confirmed by His Word. If God instructs you to do something, He will repeat, just as He did with His disciples. Jesus will always speak because He loves us; all we need to do is listen.

When you hear His voice, be sure to act on it. Don't be like the disciples who heard Jesus' instruction yet kept falling asleep. Take Him seriously the first time because His guidance is far more valuable to obey than the weak desires of our flesh.

Also, remaining awake to God's assignment is far more exciting when you know that He is clear and specific with His instruction. Sometimes, however, God's voice may seem silent or faint, and His direction lacks detail, which can be challenging. Think of the disciples: I can imagine being told to stay up and pray with no further information, which made sleep even more appealing to them.

Sometimes, we are like that; we want God to tell us to "Do this because of that," not realizing that we don't need to know the full picture. We only need to follow His instructions and trust Him.

Remaining awake leads to fruitfulness. Jesus gives us direction and rewards us when we obey him. God's Word says that Jesus is the vine, and we are the branches; we only bear fruit and succeed in life when we remain connected to Him (***The Holy Bible, New International Version,*** **2011/1973, John 15:5**). It's only in and through Him, and by following Jesus' Word, that we bear fruit. Knowing this makes obedience worthwhile—no matter how difficult.

Ultimately, we stay awake because doing what God says is far more fulfilling than staying asleep. The disciples missed a chance to prepare for the trial ahead. If we fail to do our part, we miss out on the wisdom and joy found in Him. Of course, we don't want to miss out, and there are ways for us to stay awake when God instructs.

Deny Selfish Ambition: Align Yourself to God's Will

Exhaustion, stress, burnout, and stagnation are sometimes symptoms of misalignment with God's will. When we try to build our lives without consulting Him, we gain temporary progress and satisfaction, but the second we get tired, everything comes crashing down. Yet, when we make God's will the center of our decisions and steps in life, we minimize the risk of straying from Him.

Being aligned with God's will puts everything in its rightful place. He holds the plan and outcome in His hands, so when we tire, we can rest comfortably in Him—knowing He works everything out for good (***The Holy Bible, New International Version,* 2011/1973, Romans 8:28**).

Plans that are misaligned to God's will don't take us far. We may be successful, but we'll never appreciate that success. We'll likely feel drained or unfulfilled by life. But when we continually prioritize God and His plans for us, things change. We become content, no matter the outcome.

Living in obedience to God's will is freeing. This doesn't mean things will go smoothly or be easy, but we can trust God to help us through the challenges we face. Whenever we feel misaligned with God's will, we can always turn to the Bible for comfort. We can also use Scripture to pray ourselves back into alignment.

- "Direct my footsteps according to your word; let no sin rule over me" (***The Holy Bible, New International Version,* 2011/1973, Psalm 119:133**).

- "He has shown you, O mortal, what is good. And what does the Lord require of you? To act justly and to love mercy and to walk humbly with your God" (***The Holy Bible, New International Version,* 2011/1973, Micah 6:8**).

- "This is the confidence we have in approaching God: that if we ask anything according to his will, he hears us" (***The Holy Bible, New International Version,* 2011/1973, 1 John 5:14**).

We can't risk being distant from God by casually fitting Him into our day. We need to start declaring His will over our lives in prayer. Seek Him first and put His desire for us at the center of everything we do—that's how we stay awake. The truth is, we struggle if we don't align ourselves with God's will. Had the disciples kept Jesus' will for them at the forefront of their minds at that moment in Gethsemane, they would have stayed awake and done as He had instructed.

To align ourselves with God's will, we must seek wisdom from Him (**Rotzoll, n.d.**). As **James 1:5** highlights, God will give us wisdom when we lack it, and He does so generously and without fault. Jesus does not withhold what can bring us closer to Him and make us more fruitful. Once you are aligned with His will, you need to surrender to it. Surrender looks like staying awake when Jesus instructs it. Go to God in prayer and ask for wisdom to know His will for you. Also, ask for the strength to follow it.

Practice Self-Control Not to Fall Into Temptation

Self-control is one of the fruits of the Spirit, as named in **Galatians 5:22–23**. This means the Holy Spirit enables us to practice discipline, master our emotions, act with a sound mind, and exercise willpower. The fruits of the Spirit start with love and end with self-control. It is a fruit that undergirds all the others. The Lord gifted us self-control, love, and power, and we should live according to that truth (*The Holy Bible, New International Version,* **2011/1973, 2 Timothy 1:7**). Control temptations, unhelpful impulses, and negative emotions. Doing so increases the possibility of living a patient, kind, and loving life.

God wants our minds, hearts, and bodies to be devoted to His will, and self-control helps us do that. To further facilitate the fruits of the spirit, we should practice some spiritual disciplines, including prayer, fasting, quiet time, regularly reading Scripture, serving, tithing, and memorizing God's Word.

We need to live within certain boundaries that keep our spirit awake to what God is saying at all times, especially as believers. This requires us to practice self-control. People in the pen are meant to be examples to those outside, demonstrating God's goodness in everything. Recognize your areas of weakness and practice surrendering them to God. Self-control centers our lives around God's plans, love, grace, and goodness, rather than our selfish ambitions. With it, we begin to create healthy habits that keep us open to God's transformative power in our lives. Self-control awakens us to persistently live out the principles that Jesus embodies.

Stay passionate for Christ, be Holy Spirit-dependent, think correctly, and have boundaries. Your passion for Christ will keep you on fire for His will. Contrary to popular belief, living within parameters as a self-controlled person isn't devoid of emotion and fun. You can still be a passionate person. But instead of being led by ungodly desires, your passion and self-control are rooted in God's will.

Also, practice self-control by being Holy Spirit-dependent. God must be your guide, and there's simply no other way to avoid temptation, just as Jesus cautioned the disciples to stay awake to prevent falling into temptation. The flesh was too weak for the disciples to stay up in their own strength. Similarly, when we are Holy Spirit-dependent, we rely solely on Jesus' power to keep us focused, obedient, and spiritually awake.

Another way to maintain self-control is by changing how you think. Sometimes, our thoughts keep us stuck in patterns that block us from discernment. Perhaps you are asleep because your thoughts are misleading you. By meditating on the Bible, we can change our minds to focus on God's will and instruction. God's Word demonstrates how we must think and live. This way, you remain within the boundaries of what He wants for you.

Keep Your Eyes Open and Stay Watchful

Philippians 1:9–11 is part of a thanksgiving prayer that highlights the need for discernment. Verses 9 and 10 read as follows, "And this is my prayer: that your love may abound more and more in knowledge and depth of insight, so that you may be able to discern what is best and may be pure and blameless for the day of Christ," (***The Holy Bible, New International Version,*** 2011/1973, Philippians 1:9–10).

Keeping our eyes open and staying watchful is about discerning what is appropriate and acceptable to God. Living with open eyes and being discerning keeps us alert to what's coming. This is the instruction Jesus shared with His disciples. We are expected to pray as a way to stay awake. When we pray, we actively engage with God, and He reveals what we need to know.

The helpful gift of discernment can be used in many situations. It allows us to evaluate areas of our lives and choices, helping us understand the spiritual rewards or consequences associated with them. Discernment isn't a skill that matures overnight. To develop it, we must be attentive to God's Word, obey, and understand the Good Shepherd's desire for us.

Ephesians 6:12 clearly states that we do not battle against flesh and blood but struggle against rulers, principalities, and authorities of the dark world. We should keep our eyes open so we don't fall into the traps of being deceived by these powers and spiritual forces. Social media, music, entertainment, news, and blogs are often influenced by these powers. Stay awake, prayerful, and watchful so God can show you what to avoid scrolling through.

The Bible has many examples of keeping eyes open and staying watchful; Matthew 26:36–46 isn't the only one. We see this in Deuteronomy 4:15, when the Israelites are commanded to watch themselves closely so they don't become idolatrous. Again, in the book of Psalms, it is written that we wake up daily so we can remain watchful and meditate on God's promises (***The Holy Bible, New International Version,*** **2011/1973, Psalm 119:14**8). As Jesus' sheep, who are susceptible to sleep, we meditate on His Word, and His guidance is how we keep our eyes open.

God's Word also reiterates that we should always be on the lookout and remain prayerful (***The Holy Bible, New International Version,*** **2011/1973, Luke 21:36)**. We are instructed today, just as the disciples were back then, to walk in this truth.

Living with our eyes open involves seeing how God sees and doing things as He instructs. We need discernment to distinguish the Good Shepherd's voice, which tries to lead us, from the enemy's voice, which tries to distract and destroy us. Additional examples of discernment are found in the Bible, including **Romans 12:2**, which instructs us to be cautious of conformity. We are told not to conform to the ways of the world—the trends, cultures, and thinking patterns.

Instead, we are encouraged to be mentally transformed by knowing and assessing God's will. Also, in Hebrews 4:12, the Bible tells us that God's Word is living and active, "sharper than any double-edged sword" (*The Holy Bible, New International Version,* 2011/1973, **Hebrews 4:**12). It pierces through any confusion, deception, and division. We can discern thoughts and the heart's intentions with God's Word living and active within us.

Matthew 7:1 instructs us not to judge others, and a large part of that is because judgment clouds how we approach people. Instead of approaching them in love, as the golden rule of the Bible instructs, we approach them with animosity. So, the key to discernment is nonjudgment. The Bible shows that both Jesus' ministry and discernment are matters of the heart. This is nonnegotiable. Our hearts need to be turned to all things pure and pleasing to God—judgment is not one of those things.

Also, if we want discernment, we must ask God for it in prayer. As the book of Psalms demonstrates, we can speak directly to God and say: "Lord, I am your servant; give me discernment that I may understand your statutes" (*The Holy Bible, New International Version,* **2011/1973, Psalm 119:125**). No one else can provide real spiritual awakening and understanding but Him.

Remember His Power at Work in You

Jesus sustains us. He enables us to do the impossible and transforms us to be like Him. It is written that we should surrender every aspect of our lives to Him, for He is able to do incredibly more in our lives than we could ever think or ask of Him (*The Holy Bible, New International Version,* 2011/1973, **Ephesians 3:**21). We remain awake by recognizing that the Good Shepherd doesn't leave us. His power is at work in us at all times.

Knowing that Jesus works in us is such an encouraging revelation. God's glory is upon us now, not tomorrow or when we get to Heaven, but today. And that's why we can marvel at His goodness. In moments of weakness, when we struggle to stay awake on our own, we can call on His power.

Another aspect of remembering His power at work in us is not forgetting Him once we've received the miracle. Too often, we don't build on what God has already shown us. Our trust in Him should be based on what we already know of Him. This will help us remember His goodness, even in troubling times.

Consider the story of the 10 lepers whom Jesus healed in **Luke 17:11–19**. In this story, 10 men with leprosy needed healing and asked Jesus for it. When Jesus provided the healing they needed, only one of the ten men returned to thank Him in remembrance of what He had done. The other nine men went on their way, enjoying the healing but forgetting the Healer. Let's not be like them.

We can do all things through the Good Shepherd, including awakening from spiritual sleep. But as we remember Jesus' power at work in us, we should praise Him for who He is and what He does. Though our flesh is weak, the Holy Spirit is not overwhelmed by anything; He gives us the strength to overcome. The apostle Paul understood this and wasn't ashamed of proclaiming that the Holy Spirit can achieve supernatural results in us. He can even keep us up when our bodies are falling asleep.

We only need to remember His power at work in us. We need to become more conscious of Christ's power and eternal might, which is moving things around in and for you. Jesus is full in areas where we are empty, so we can trust Him to be faithful. Meditating on God's Word and staying prayerful is how we live in remembrance of His power. In Christ, we can bear anything and overcome all things.

Have the Mindset Christ Had in Gethsemane

In the garden of Gethsemane, Jesus was faithful to go a little further and pray (***The Holy Bible, New International Version,*** **2011/1973,**

Matthew 26:39). He was persistent in prayer, knowing the pain that was inevitably coming. The Good Shepherd must be an example to us. To have the mindset Christ had in Gethsemane is to pray continuously. Bring all you have and all you lack to God.

Staying awake when you're drifting into sleep is hard. But in Gethsemane, Jesus recognized that the hard thing needed to be done. He did not step out of obedience to satisfy the flesh. Instead, He pushed forward, strengthening the Spirit in His obedience. That's what the Gethsemane mindset embodies. We need to push past fleshly desires by the power of Jesus at work in us. This way, the Spirit is exercised and further strengthened.

Even with dread and impending agony, Christ carried out His mission. He could have stopped His suffering at any point, but He chose to remain faithful to His word for the sake of His Holy name and our salvation. We ought to be doers, too. We shouldn't just say we want to walk up from spiritual sleep, but we need to act on it. Read the Bible, repent, ask God for discernment, walk in obedience, and pray. Let us not be people who go back on their word, falling asleep when we've agreed to stay awake with God. Instead, let's embody the mindset of persistence and follow through as Christ did in Gethsemane.

Thanks to Jesus' dedication, we are able to receive His salvation today. Think of all the people tied to our faithfulness on this journey. Some of our friends and family members will come to know the Good Shepherd through us. So we shouldn't take spiritual sleep lightly; it doesn't only affect us but also those who are meant to encounter the Lord through our testimony. Let us not be lukewarm in our devotion to God's kingdom. Let us be people who pursue Him, fully awake and discerning what's coming. It's important to be people who keep watch for their families, friends, and colleagues and pray. Staying spiritually awake by having the Gethsemane mindset is one of the best ways to support the people we care about.

Our responsibility is to remain spiritually awake to receive Jesus' instruction. There's a weight that lifts off us, knowing that Jesus is in control and all we need to do is stay connected to Him. The Good Shepherd will get us where we need to go and help us discern what we need to know. So stay alert, wait for His instruction, and don't sleep on what you are called to do. Jesus' sheep not only follow, stray, and sleep, but they also run. Some of us are at full speed, going toward things outside God's will for us. We are bolting in search of what the enemy wants us to believe we can't find within the pen.

But what does running look like? Why do we run? And what does Jesus have to say about this? Let's unpack these questions in the next chapter. For those who can already tell that they are running from God, don't worry—there's no place where His love won't find you.

Chapter 6:

Jesus' Sheep—Run

Physical running improves our health and overall vitality, but spiritual running does the opposite. When we run from the pen, we run from God's provision, protection, and presence. Though there's nowhere we can go to escape from Him because He is omnipresent, there are things we can do to distance ourselves from Him. Running is one of those things.

Jesus' sheep run. It's a common human behavior. We may do so because we don't feel worthy of Jesus' unconditional love, or because we don't want to do what the Good Shepherd instructs. The book of Jonah reveals a lot about running, why we do it, and how God responds to it. In the book, God calls Jonah to preach in Nineveh, a sinful city of antiquity (**Stone, 2019**). Instead of heeding this call and preaching in Nineveh as God instructed, Jonah chose disobedience by running from the call.

Jonah loathed the Assyrians, Israel's enemy, who lived in Nineveh. It probably felt unreal to him that God instructed him to preach to the very city he detested. Jonah ran out of his own desires, but that landed him in a far tougher situation than if he had just obeyed God.

Running from His call led Jonah to a ship with skilled sailors, who soon experienced the consequences of his poor decision. While on the ship, God made the waves crash so violently that "the sailors were afraid and each cried out to his own god" (***The Holy Bible, New International Version,*** **2011/1973, Jonah 1:4–5**). During this time, Jonah was fast asleep below the ship's deck.

Perplexed, the captain of the ship woke Jonah up, asking how he could sleep through such turbulence. Everyone aboard the ship was afraid for their lives, but Jonah was resting because he knew the responsibility for the unrest was on him. He ran, so trouble followed him onto the ship.

Sometimes, we know that we are running from God's call when we bring trouble to the places we run to, and the people around us bear the consequences.

The story of Jonah's running is in chapter 1, verses 1 through 17, and it offers a great perspective on what we tend to do when we know God is calling us to do something different. It also reveals how God reacts to our disobedience, especially when it gets in the way of bringing other sheep into the pen.

Why Run?

Bitterness and sin are two of many possible reasons why people run from God. Having an unforgiving heart when our Creator calls us to be forgiving is a sign of disobedience. And not wanting to submit to God's call makes us want to run away from it. Similarly, sin keeps us in a state of self-gratification. We'd rather do what we want than respond to what the Good Shepherd wants for us.

You may have your own reasons for running. Perhaps you've placed worldly standards on what God can do. For example, if your earthly father hurt you, you may transfer that hurt onto your Heavenly Father. Perhaps you don't feel worthy of God's calling on your life, so you run to prevent your biggest fears from materializing. The fear of humiliation, failure, and disappointing God are all very real reasons why people run.

Like Jonah, we may fear obeying what God calls us to. Sometimes, we find it hard to trust what's on the other side of God's calling for our lives. So we stall following His instruction, and when we see that He is true to His word, we feel panicked and attempt to escape His instruction.

However, God remains faithful and does not forsake us despite our running. The good news is that there's nothing we can or cannot do that surprises God. Our shortcomings don't discredit us from God's desire to fulfill His purpose for our lives.

Also, God loves us so much that He is willing to forgive us no matter how many times we fall, as long as we turn back to Him and repent. God loves us too much to let us sit in a place of shame and hurt for too long. He even provided for and protected Jonah during a self-imposed storm, shielding him in the belly of an enormous fish. Loving-kindness is just part of His nature. And because He is kind, He is aware of why we run, yet He still pursues and cares for us.

A Bitter, Unforgiving Heart

There are multiple reasons why Jesus' sheep run from God. It can be bitterness or unforgiveness, even though we are encouraged to forgive as the Father has forgiven us (and continuously forgives us). The Bible is clear that we need to be compassionate to people, forgiving them as Jesus has forgiven us (***The Holy Bible, New International Version, 2011/1973, Ephesians 4:32***). But when we choose to do the opposite—decide to be unkind and unforgiving—we find ourselves running from God.

Jesus doesn't want bitterness for us. The Bible actually teaches the importance of forgiveness. If we forgive people, God will also forgive us (***The Holy Bible, New International Version, 2011/1973, Matthew 6:14***). Unforgiveness prevents us from receiving what God has for us. It hardens our hearts to the point where goodness and kindness can no longer permeate through us.

Bitterness doesn't lead to salvation; it leads to judgment (**Piper, 1988**). When we allow resentment and unforgiveness to dwell in our hearts, it takes root and becomes something that poisons us against ourselves. A seed grows in us from bitterness and becomes an unforgiving spirit that leads us to destruction.

Instead of allowing bitterness to take root in our hearts, we should trust God to fight for us. Many a time, bitterness develops when someone wrongs us. We fall into the mentality of needing to punish those who have lied, hurt, stolen, or rejected us. We may even ruminate over the transgressions to justify our bitterness. The thing is, no matter how correct we might be about the injustice someone has done toward us, we are called to forgive. Think about it. Even some of Jesus' final words on the cross were, "Father, forgive them, for they do not know what they are doing" (***The Holy Bible, New International Version, 2011/1973, Luke 23:34***). He demonstrated forgiveness by interceding for the very people who persecuted Him.

We are not meant to spend our days plotting our revenge because God will work it out. He is against injustice and doesn't let it go unaddressed so we can trust Him. We typically run from the pen when we feel we can do it better than Christ or He won't fight for us. But the Bible is clear that He is our defender. We only need to be still and let Him intercede for us.

Jonah ran from God because he didn't have a forgiving heart toward the Assyrians of Nineveh. When God instructed him to preach there, he was consumed by a bitter heart, running from the very thing he was called to do. We also become like that sometimes.

We choose to lose relationships and friendships because we assume ourselves to be "right" and label the next person as "wrong." However, we are often called to forgive and reconcile with people. The Good Shepherd cares more about our obedience to His command of forgiveness. He wants better for us, so we gain more if we humble ourselves and obey Him.

Living in Sin

Another reason people run from God is sin. When we talk about living in sin, we refer to perpetually breaking commandments. It's living in such a way that the world recognizes us, but Jesus doesn't. Sin is a recurring theme associated with everything that pulls us away from the pen. Living in sin and sin itself is God's enemy. It will always beckon us to step outside His will for our lives. We can't live purposefully when we constantly follow and live in sin.

Sin has been normalized and engrained in society for so long now. It's almost trendy to step outside of what God calls us to do and choose to live sinfully. But we weren't created to be slaves to sin or to conform to the ways of this world. We are called to be different and to choose things that align with God's will for us.

Living in sin puts a barrier between us and the Good Shepherd. Sin pulls us away from fellowship and directs us toward shame. **Isaiah 59:2** confirms that a sinful life hides God's face from us and separates us from Him. This is not a barrier we want to have in our lives.

Thankfully, our sin doesn't mean Jesus wants nothing to do with us, even though it should. Jesus shows us compassion and gives us grace for our sinful ways. The Good Shepherd could have turned His back on us because we live in sin, but He chose to restore us. In Christ, we have daily opportunities to repent of our sin and be cleansed in Him. Every day we take those opportunities, His power covers us and removes sin's hold over us.

Jesus does everything to bring us back to Him. However, if we are stuck in our ways, refusing to run back to Him, sometimes the greatest act of mercy is to give us over to our sinful desires (***The Holy Bible, New International Version,* 2011/1973, Romans 1**:24). When He does that, we feel the misery and weight of our decisions, and typically run back to Him. But even when we sin, He gently shows His love for us, hoping we'll wake up to His glory, power, and goodness.

Imagine a loving parent, as I'd like to think my wife and I are. When our daughter does something that will cause harm to her, we correct her repeatedly. However, at some point, she'll probably need to learn the hard way that certain behaviors have consequences. If Mom and Dad say, "Don't touch the hot stove," don't do it. But sometimes, the thrill of doing what we are told not to do takes over us. Suddenly, our hand is over the stove, just to feel what it's like to touch it. The natural consequence of that disobedience is burning a finger or two. That's what sin is—a hot stove we get burned on.

When Jesus says, "Don't go there" or "Don't do that," He isn't trying to be no fun. He's instructing us to protect us from what He knows sin can do. Sometimes, like children who don't listen to their parents, we learn the hard way. We go where He didn't send us and do what He instructed us not to, only to experience the natural consequences of disobedience. Even so, Jesus doesn't leave us. He offers mercy daily and multiple chances to return to Him. We can run to the Good Shepherd, just like a child who has burned their hand on a hot plate runs to their parent, crying, "Mom, Dad, my hand hurts." Jesus embraces us when we return to Him and repent. He doesn't turn us away but comforts us in the mess. We shouldn't allow sin to separate us from the Good Shepherd. Jesus loves us and dies to save us from living in sin. However, in moments when the flesh is weak and we fall prey to sinful desires, we need to confess our sins to God. We need to humble ourselves at His feet and ask for forgiveness because the longer we let sin go on, the more grip the enemy has over us.

We receive forgiveness when we turn away from sin, return to God, and acknowledge our rebellion against Him. Though we don't earn His mercy or deserve it, He is faithful to supply it, anyway. Praise the name of Jesus!

Have you ever stopped to think about your life and how much better it would be if you committed to staying in the pen rather than running into the world? There would be less confusion and more clarity, that's for sure. Maybe you should reflect on what sins make you keep up with trends rather than reading your Bible and focusing on the Good Shepherd.

What's making you run away from God's calling for your life? Once you've reflected on these things, hand them over to God. Allow yourself the opportunity to confess, repent, and be forgiven by Him daily. Also, consider the cost of those sins in the greater picture of eternity. Your decision to walk away from sinful living and back to God will transform your life.

The Truth About Running

Running from what God has called you to do creates exhaustion. It also leads to chaos all around you. Consider Jonah on the ship, sleeping from fatigue while the sea began to rage. Jonah knew the havoc was happening because he had chosen to run from God's instruction. Jonah's decision to run jeopardized the lives of all the other men on the ship. Because he was there, those men no longer felt safe on the sea as it raged. Similarly, our choices (our sinful nature) impact the safety of those around us.

When We Run, God Is With Us Wherever We Are

The thing about running from God is that there's nowhere we can hide from Him. Hebrews 4:13 clarifies that "nothing in all creation is hidden" from God; nothing is concealed from the Creator's eyes, and we must all give account for our choices (***The Holy Bible, New International Version,* 2011/1973, Hebrews 4:13**). Jonah ran, but God was watching it all. He saw him on the ship with those sailors.

God knows everything and is there for us when no one else is near or understands what we are going through. Remember, no one is closer to your situation and more understanding of it than Jesus. He felt it all and walked through it all, so you can call on Him when a need arises.

Maybe you feel you've run so far that no one would know where to find you. But Jesus knows your situation. He knows if you feel you've run too far from Him. God knows when you feel trapped. He is aware of when you sit and when you stand. If you go up into the heavens, God is there, and when you lay your head to sleep at night, He is also there (***The Holy Bible, New International Version,* 2011/1973, Psalm 139:8**). There's no distance far enough for us to run from His Spirit and presence. So turn it over to Him. Whether you are facing a new situation or a recurring stressor, let Him know because He cares—His presence is there with you.

When We Run, God Pursues Us

Today's culture is rooted in "self-love" and the concept of "finding yourself." But the Bible leads us to pursue God and accept His invitation to seek Him. Sometimes, we allow ourselves to be influenced by what the culture says, and as a result, we find ourselves going out into the world in search of "self." We launch ourselves into various literature, philosophies, and other schools of thought, running further away from God's Word in our chase. Before we know it, the culture turns us into self-proclaimed "truth seekers." Yet, in all this running and searching, we turn away from the very Truth—Jesus. Jonah thought he had run miles away in the opposite direction of where God wanted him to go, but no distance is too far.

When the all-knowing God seeks you out, as He did with Jonah, He finds you wherever you are. Jesus is the Good Shepherd because He doesn't give up on us. He could have let Jonah go on and do what he wanted, but He still sought him out. When Jonah hid or attempted to hide on the ship, God didn't choose someone else for the job. He could have chosen someone willing to answer the call, but He purposed Jonah—and only Jonah—for the mission to Nineveh. He is as relentless in His pursuit of us.

It doesn't matter where in the world we are, whether on land or sea, God always pursues us. He takes personal delight in you and me. Each sheep is special to the Good Shepherd. If there was no one else in the world but you, He would have still laid down His life for you. That's how remarkable you are to Jesus.

God pursues us because His love for us is deep. Psalm 139:17–18 puts it beautifully by saying, "How precious to me are your thoughts, God! How vast is the sum of them! Were I to count them, they would outnumber the grains of sand, when I awake, I am still with you" (*The Holy Bible, New International Version,* 2011/1973, **Psalm 139:17–18**). How remarkable it is to know that God thinks about us. His thoughts about us individually are more numerous than we could ever think in a lifetime.

When the Good Shepherd decides that He wants you to fulfill a calling, it will happen. The beauty of it all is that God pursues us despite our flaws. He chooses us because He chose us before we were even conceived, and He does not go back on His word.

When We Run, God Interrupts Our Plans

God will interrupt our lives to get us back on track. Jonah made it on the ship, and it even left the port. He probably thought he had succeeded in running. But God wasn't done with him yet. Instead of letting Jonah remain on the ship, God interrupted the trip by sending a storm. He did this not to punish Jonah for going in the opposite direction of His call but to get him back on track. God sent violent waves as a way to intervene for Jonah. He knew that His plan for Jonah was far more beneficial than his fear.

God knew that Jonah needed to be rescued from his own way of thinking, so the storm was sent to benefit him. The seas got so rough that the sailors began to cry out to the Lord for mercy as they prepared to throw Jonah off the ship (*The Holy Bible, New International Version*, **2011/1973, Jonah 1:14**). The point is that when we run, the consequences spill over.

When the sailors became aware that Jonah was responsible for the surging waters, they surrendered him into the ocean. Once Jonah was overboard, God calmed the sea, allowing the sailors to continue their voyage.

Overboard the ship, Jonah was swallowed by a whale that God had provided (*The Holy Bible, New International Version,* **2011/1973, Jonah 1**:17). He was in the belly of the fish for three days and nights until it spat him up near Nineveh—the place God initially called him to go. So, no matter how far we think we are running, God always has a plan to bring us right back to where He called us to be.

When We Run, the Storm Gets Worse

Another truth about running is the longer we run, the worse the turbulence becomes. Life throws many problems at us, and the only way to overcome them is to face them. It started in Eden when Adam and Eve disobeyed God by sinning against Him, and they ran and hid (*The Holy Bible, New International Version,* **2011/1973, Genesis 3:10**). We often do the same in our own lives.

Suppose rent is due, and you choose to run and hide from reality. Hiding won't make the problem go away. It will only make your property owner furious and increase the debt that needs to be paid. That's what happens when we run and hide from God. The turbulence in our lives doesn't ease; it simply gets worse.

When Jonah ran, a storm came to where he was. Had the sailors not tossed him overboard, the storm would have gotten worse and put everyone's lives in danger. Similarly, when God has to pursue us with no repentance or surrender on our side, things often get much worse before they get better.

Thankfully, we can never run far from God's grace. Our sin doesn't stop the Good Shepherd from pursuing us and extending His grace, just as He did for Jonah. The truth is, God's way is better. Whether it be laziness, bitterness, unforgiveness, or lack of faith causing us to resist God's calling, please remember that this resistance will also cause us to be miserable. We have the chance to turn away from misery, avoid the belly of the whale, and do exactly what God has said.

The Good Shepherd Preserves

When was the last time you felt you messed up? I mean, seriously messed up—like, "This is the biggest mistake. I'll never get back up from this" level of messed up. Perhaps you are dealing with that now, overwhelmed and full of despair. The good news is that God preserves. He hasn't forgotten you or written you off.

No matter how far we run, we cannot outrun God's purpose for our lives. Like Jonah, God made rough seas and got him swallowed by a whale to transport him back to the calling he was running from. God is faithful in keeping His promise and preserving His people. Jonah is one example. For instance, God's love motivated Him to preserve the Israelites.

Noah is also another example of how God preserves. The only difference between Noah and Jonah is that Noah listened to God for the first time. When he was instructed to build an ark, he obeyed, even when he may have looked comical to those who didn't understand his calling. Noah's story is proof of how God rewards obedience. Because Noah listened and did as God instructed, his family was saved from the flood.

The key contrast between Noah and Jonah is one did what God said, and the other ran from what He said. But the one thing that remained consistent was God's response to them. Jonah messed up and had to endure turbulence on his way back to do what he was running from, but God still stayed with him.

You see, Jesus remains with the Jonahs of this world as much as He does the Noahs. Trust Him with your life, both when things are going well and when they aren't. God has you covered. He will intervene for you, even in your messiest moments.

Even though we go through hard times and dark valleys, the Good Shepherd is faithful to preserve us. He promises to be with us every step of the way, and never leaving nor forsaking us. This should reassure us because God goes before us in our trials so we can trust Him with the hard stuff.

Because God is omnipresent, He sees our attempts to flee from His instruction. Yet, as the Good Shepherd, He does what He can to preserve us so we may reach our purpose.

Much like Jonah, we can make poor decisions in life by trying to run and hide from what God wants. Fortunately, the Good Shepherd has already accounted for our behaviors as His sheep. He already knows that Jesus' Sheep can stray and attempt to run away. Because He is the Good Shepherd, He has already made provisions for our mistakes and poor choices.

His goodness and mercy follow us all the days of our lives (**Psalm 23:**6), and His grace is sufficient for us (**2 Corinthians 12:9**). God's favor and preservation don't depend on us; they're solely reliant on His character. Since God is consistent and true to His word, He freely gives His favor to us.

Even our mistakes don't prevent God's preservation. There are things we do we are not proud of. We make numerous choices that are risky and unnecessary. Sometimes, these decisions lead to financial, emotional, and psychological strife. Needless to say, we experience the consequences of those decisions. But God holds nothing against us. He is there, even when we make the worst decisions in life—like running from His instructions.

God could have let Jonah drown in the rough sea with those sailors on the boat that day, but He didn't. Instead, He caused turbulence to push Jonah back into a righteous journey with Him. God preserved Jonah's life on the boat and as he was thrown into the sea.

Then, the Good Shepherd further preserved Jonah's purpose by keeping him in the belly of the whale for three days so he could get spat out in Nineveh, where his calling was. We see from Jonah's story that God isn't waiting for us to get our act together or become sheep that don't run. Rather, He is committed to what He has spoken and preserves our lives because He is sovereign and wants the best for us.

Jonah's story shows God's sovereignty in our lives. His hand is so much bigger than anything we experience that He can bring us back on track in one swoop. The Good Shepherd's will for us is rooted in recognizing His reign and commandments, no matter which season we are in.

Jesus did not come to judge us or isolate us because we are human and fall victim to fear. Instead, He came to free us so that we may still experience the fullness of life and run toward His purpose, regardless of fearfulness. That, in itself, is a form of preservation.

If you are battling with questions right now or have found yourself running from the Good Shepherd, don't despair. It's never too late to run back to Him. God provides a path that leads you back to where He has destined you to go. He did it with Jonah, and God has no favorites—He will do it with us. Destiny is not something you choose for yourself, but it's God's will. He knows, even before you do, what you are supposed to do. Jonah was fighting his original calling, but God led him back.

Fear: A Barrier to Obedience

The enemy likes to weaponize fear against us. Sometimes we get so afraid of following through on what God has called us to that we lean into disobeying him. Fear is a barrier to executing God's call over our lives. It is one of the things that keeps us running from the Good Shepherd. When fear is weaponized against us, it becomes a barrier to our obedience, and the enemy knows this. This is why the Bible reminds us that the Lord is with us, holding our right hand, saying, "Do not fear, I will help you" (***The Holy Bible, New International***

Version, 2011/1973, Isaiah 41:13). We can choose to discern the Good Shepherd's voice and obey Him. Once we submit to God, we have authority in Jesus to denounce the enemy and the fear that comes with him. To overcome fear, we must remember that God has given us a strong spirit of power, love, and self-discipline (***The Holy Bible, New International Version,*** **2011/1973, 2 Timothy 1:**7). This means we can be headstrong in our decision to override fear and lean on Jesus. Also, obeying what God calls us to do often alleviates fear.

Think of Jonah. He was probably afraid of being in the belly of the whale. However, he could have prevented that period by obeying God's instructions. We all have a duty to perform, a good deed placed in the spirit, and a talent needed for something important to be fulfilled. The only issue is when we run from the way God wants us to use all that He has placed within us.

Dear friend, be courageous in your life and do not fear. Bring your fear under God's authority. Focus on what God wants for and asks of you, not on your fear. Even when Jonah told the men on the ship to throw him overboard because his disobedience was causing chaos, he said it with ease. He knew the storm wouldn't harm him because he was returning to God's call for him.

People tend to think and respond to fear in the moment. They don't consider the long-term effects of the decision and how it will shape the lives of those around them. When it comes to obeying God, don't let fear overcome you, as it initially did with Jonah. Perhaps there's something you don't feel prepared for, but you are well aware that God is calling you to do it. Be empowered to walk by faith in His Word and not by sight. The enemy uses fear to distract you from your purpose, but God is your helper, so leave your fear at His feet.

The Lord Sent That

Since we cannot outrun God's purpose for us, He will send interruptions to redirect us. For Jonah, it was the storm that threw him off the boat and into the belly of a whale. At the end of the day, the truth remains unshaken: God will do as He pleases, and His purpose will stand (*The Holy Bible, New International Version,* 2011/1973, **Isaiah 46:10**).

The Bible clearly states that "In their hearts humans plan their course, but the Lord establishes their steps" (*The Holy Bible, New International Version,* 2011/1973, **Proverbs 16:9**). Jonah decided not to go to Nineveh; instead, he planned to sleep on the ship until he reached his preferred destination, thinking his plans were unraveling. But God's plan prevailed, just as it does in our lives.

In the belly of the whale, Jonah realized that he really needed to trust God's purpose for him. Sometimes, for things to get better, they first need to get worse. The sailors witnessed God's power and converted to believing in Him. This is a testimony of how God can use your bad choices to save you and those around you for the glory of His name. The Good Shepherd is constantly pursuing us.

God's providence for the Jonahs of this world is unshaken. If you are Jonah in this season, even though you promised yourself you'd do better, I'd like you to remember the following truths—God will turn your mistake into His glory if you can, like Jonah, admit, "This storm was my doing." The Lord sends the storm and the whale for your good and redirection.

Of course, you should accept your choices and their consequences, but never should you believe that God will leave you there alone. The Good Shepherd was with Jonah on the ship, with him as he was tossed into the raging sea, and with him in the belly of the whale. Sure, you'll need to face your decisions because God is too good to keep you from the growth those lessons bring. He will not leave you to go through the challenges alone. Your mistakes, sins, and reckless choices don't disqualify you from God's plan. He will use them for good and give you testimonies that point to His goodness. Your mistakes will not change God's love for you—His love for you is eternal.

The Good Shepherd has a plan for you, and you can never stop it, even if you run from Him. Whatever events are unfolding around you, God is for you; He is with you and beside you. Find hope in the fact that He redeems and rescues His beloved, even from their own actions.

The Window of Change

Jonah spent three days in the belly of the whale before being spat out in Nineveh, where he was called to go. Sometimes, what we fear is actually our destiny, and the challenges are the window through which God is trying to change us.

What is your Nineveh? Is it avoiding forgiveness or reconciliation with people in your life? Pick up the phone and step out of the cycle of avoidance. Your life should demonstrate the heart of God for His people.

Write things down and ask God to help you go toward your Nineveh instead of running from it. Instead of running away, run toward the Good Shepherd.

God created us with and for a purpose. Sometimes, He intervenes and pushes us out of our comfort zones so our purpose is fulfilled. If it were up to us, we would be like Jonah, resting in comfort rather than working in obedience. But the Good Shepherd cares about what we do, so He pushes us out of what could lead to spiritual sleep. The Lord always helps us walk in purpose.

But this hurts; why is He calling me? This might be a question in your mind when you go through seasons of God-sending situations to get you out of comfort. The answer is, God sends the turbulence so you can ride the storm toward Him. He calls you and qualifies you for the process. He does all of this so you can transform from within and be equipped for eternity with him.

Maybe you are dealing with a version of being in the belly of a whale, meaning trouble has found you in this season. Perhaps the best way to get through it is to submit yourself. Don't fight God's purpose and calling over your life. Follow His path and redirection because both are ways for you to return to Him. Returning to Him might not be easy when we run from the Good Shepherd. It can look as messy as Jonah's journey back. But every bad thing leads to an even better thing because the Good Shepherd cares for us.

Blessed be the name of the Lord, for even when we try to run, His mercy meets us where we are and brings us back home. That's why we need Him. If we aren't following, straying, or running, then Jesus' sheep are falling. But who cares this much for us and will keep picking us up and bringing us back to our calling and purpose? The Good Shepherd will.

Chapter 7:

Jesus' Sheep—Fall

Jesus is never surprised when we fall; He is always prepared for it—just as He was when Peter denied Him three times. The Scripture of focus is Mark **14:27–31**, where Jesus foresees Peter's fall. But when Jesus tells Peter this, he insists he would die alongside the Good Shepherd before ever denying Him.

Sometimes, we are like Peter. We may feel settled in the pen and comfy next to Jesus, thinking we are close, but in reality, we've drifted away from Him. We've embraced complacency. Perhaps we no longer read the Bible, and His Word no longer informs our choices. Sometimes, falling looks like praying for convenience rather than a genuine relationship or only going to Jesus as a fictional character goes to a genie to "make a wish." Maybe, like Peter, there was a time in our own lives when we truly believed we were following Jesus, but fear or other distractions overwhelmed, making us act outside of His will.

When the time came to deny Jesus, Peter was afraid of being identified as a disciple, so he did all he could to blend into the crowd as the guards took Jesus away (**Thompson, 2021**). Sometimes, our denial of Jesus doesn't stop at distancing ourselves from Him by not reading the Bible or praying, but it continues into our daily choices. Maybe we are in a season where proclaiming Jesus' name isn't trendy or "cool" for our lives right now, so we deny Him by blending into the world. Perhaps we are too afraid to say we are interested in a relationship with Jesus, lest we come across as "weirdos" or "boring" to our friends and those around.

Many times, like Peter, we try to fit into groups that aren't receptive to the Good Shepherd. Some of us are believers who aren't open about our faith, to the point where people are surprised when they learn we are Christians. Others are seekers who are curious about God and may desire a relationship with the Creator. But we are too scared of how pursuing righteousness will look to the people we've spent our lives sinning with. We may fall into a pattern of gossip, hiding, and outright denying Jesus just for clicks or popularity. Sometimes, the flesh gets the best of us, as it did Peter, and we don't die for what we said we would. Instead, we live a life of deception and selfish ambition.

It's easy to be courageous people who seek Christ behind closed doors but quickly hide the evidence when the world is around. Our walk in faith needs more than private convictions. We need to be a people who can stand firm in their decision to follow Jesus. If we aren't there yet, we need to stand firm in our decision to keep searching for Him until we get to the point of believing. We can't afford to be deniers of the Good Shepherd.

The Shepherd's Goodness When We Fall

Thankfully, Jesus is good. He is prepared for us to fall, so He makes a plan for us. First, we see that Jesus warns Peter of what's to come: "Tonight—before the rooster crows twice you yourself will disown me three times" (***The Holy Bible, New International Version, 2011/1973, Mark 14:30***). Jesus knows exactly when and why we fall, and sometimes He will warn us before it happens. Instead of taking what Jesus said to heart, Peter was prideful in responding, "Even if I have to die with you, I will never disown you" (***The Holy Bible, New International Version, 2011/1973, Mark 14:31***).

In some instances, we are like Peter—too prideful and sure about where we believe we stand with Jesus, and we fail to heed His warning. However, even though the warning shows His genuine love and care for us, Jesus doesn't stop there. Because He loves us, the Good Shepherd makes provisions for when our prideful hearts fall into the trap He warned us about.

In John 21:15-17, we see Jesus show His love for Peter not by humiliating him for having denied Him three times, but by asking him if he loves Him. In fact, the title of this passage is "Jesus Reinstates Peter" (***The Holy Bible, New International Version, 2011/1973,***

John 21). Peter denies Jesus three times but still isn't exempt from His love. Wow, how incredible is the Good Shepherd to invite us back when we fall!

Just like the grace extended to Peter, Jesus doesn't discard us when we fall. He reinstates us into the pen so we can resume a relationship with Him. With repentant hearts and willingness to let Him transform us, Jesus changes us for His name's sake, turning our fall into something much better and bigger than we could have imagined. Jesus restores us.

Our Fall Is Not Failure

All of Jesus' sheep will fall at some point in their lives. Peter denied Jesus three times—he never thought he would fall, but he face-planted. Many of us have similar areas where we think, *I'd never do that*, and then it happens. As well-intentioned as we are, Jesus' sheep fall.

Like Peter, we get ahead of ourselves. Sometimes, we have to fall so we can gain wisdom from what we've been through. Your faith is strengthened in the testing. You can say you believe in God, but when the test comes, it will truly confirm whether you have faith or not.

Even when you fall, depending on how you respond, it's not failure to fall. The Good Shepherd has grace and is always willing to offer chances for sheep who fall. The Bible says, "Do not gloat over me, my enemy! Though I have fallen, I will rise. Though I sit in darkness, the Lord will be my light" (***The Holy Bible, New International Version, 2011/1973, Micah 7:8***). Jesus is with us, even when we fall. He is our light during times of trial and helps us rise again.

Falling Is Not Failure, It's Preparation

God is not done with us. No matter how far we fall, His hand is faithful and big enough to reach out to us. If anything, the fall is preparation. God always uses the fall as fertile ground for growing something beautiful in our lives. Through the fall, He prepares us to hold the blessings that come. So, we should never despise the fall or feel like nothing good can come from it because God consistently does the impossible. In all honesty, the fall can embolden us to draw closer to Jesus and build His kingdom.

When Jesus said the disciples would fall away and "the sheep would be scattered," they had no idea the test that would come when Jesus was no longer physically present with them (*The Holy Bible, New International Version,* **2011/1973, Mark 14:27**). That's when they truly realized the frailty of their faith.

God uses the fall to prepare us for something greater. Suppose you're someone who despises and persecutes Christians. I'm sure at no point do you expect or even care to be rescued by God. Harming believers was Saul's fall. Jesus confronted Saul in his pit because every time he hurt believers, the Good Shepherd felt pain.

Saul's fall brought him to a very powerful encounter with Jesus. It propelled him to realize that everything he had innately believed about the insignificance of God and His people was wrong. He witnessed the resurrected Christ on the road to Damascus, which legitimized Jesus to him.

Years later, Jesus appointed Saul as the apostle Paul, who now has an unwavering understanding of believers as "the body of Christ," each one of us (*The Holy Bible, New International Version,* **2011/1973, 1 Corinthians 12:27)**. Paul's story and transformation speak to the power Jesus has to turn things around for us. No matter how bad your fall may be, Christ can turn it for good!

Falling Is Not Failure, It's a Chance to Practice Humility

The fall is humbling. Let's reflect on Peter, who tried to think of himself as the one disciple who would *never* fall away from Jesus but ended up being the one to disown Him three times. That's a moment of humility. We also have our own blind spots, where we believe we are better because we commit one sin, compared to someone who commits them all. However, like Peter, we are not better than anyone.

In fact, we have all sinned and fallen short of God's glory—there's no difference between us (***The Holy Bible, New International Version, 2011/1973, Romans 3:22–23).*** That's why we need the Good Shepherd to lead and rescue us.

God's Word tells us to humble ourselves by His side, and He will lift us (***The Holy Bible, New International Version,*** 2011/1973, **James 4**:**10**). We live in an ego-consumed world where pride and arrogance can be at the center of everything we do. Even Peter had his moment of pride when he told Jesus he would never betray Him. We have moments like Peter had when Jesus tells us something, but our ego says something else. Thus, we end up falling, which becomes an opportunity for humility.

Without God, we have nothing figured out. It's like we are wandering endlessly and aimlessly, but with Him, we have direction. Praise the Lord that He doesn't allow our fall and pride to keep us from His glory. The fall helps us realize that we have no answers and we don't know as much as we think we do. Practicing humility removes the blinders that prevent us from following Jesus. We are able to give Him glory for being far greater than anything we could ever do in our own strength.

Biblical humility is the fear of the Lord (***The Holy Bible, New International Version,*** 2011/1973, **Proverbs 22**:4). This isn't about being afraid of the Good Shepherd, but about remembering that He is all-powerful. God is greater than anything we could ever go through. It's recognizing that He deserves all the glory, praise, and honor.

Pride often says, "I can do this myself," so it pushes God away. When we are prideful, it becomes a barrier to our faith and stands in the way of grace. The Bible says pride comes before destruction and haughtiness before a fall (***The Holy Bible, New International Version,*** 2011/1973, **Proverbs 16:18**). It's foolish to think we can do anything without the Good Shepherd leading us. Unless God delivers us from this foolishness, we will always insist on falling away from Him. Humility reminds us that we should not put ourselves in Christ's position. It's accepting God's direction and letting Him lead us. We shouldn't fall into the trap of believing we can do it all, sidelining the One who *actually can*.

We should accept our dependence on God wholeheartedly. Our very lives exist because God breathed life into us. When we fall, it reminds us of how little control we have over our lives. It's a reminder of how necessary submission, modesty, and obedience to God are.

Falling Is Not Failure, It Exposes Our Need for Salvation

Deliverance, or being rescued from eternal suffering, is salvation, and Jesus gives it to us (**Leake, 2022**). The Good Shepherd came to save us from the everlasting penalty of sin. When we think about salvation, it's beneficial to think of it as sheep being saved from the pit by Christ, our Good Shepherd. It is an ongoing type of rescue—one we experience in the past, present, and future.

"Salvation presupposes sin" (**Anderson, 2017**). Without us falling, there would be no need for redemption. When we fall, it exposes our need for salvation—and ultimately, our need for God. Since salvation is found in Jesus alone, it is our sin that humbles us to see how limited we are as people. When our need for salvation is exposed in the fall, we seek God's limitlessness to intercede in our situation. In our redemption, God receives all the glory and praise.

Without salvation, we are spiritually lost, blind, and dead (**Mitchum, 2021**). But Jesus came for us so we may become found, watchful, and alive! Jesus is our redeemer, and God created us to live intimately with Him. Everything we experience and is not by accident—these are all situations He uses to point us back to His sovereignty and love. To have access to God's presence is a blessing. We get to fellowship with Him and experience restoration in Christ.

Falling Is Not Failure, It Builds Our Faith

When we fall into a pit, the only way out is up. Sometimes, the fall inspires us to refocus our attention toward the Good Shepherd and away from this world and its problems. We fall and suddenly realize that the only way out—and the only way to survive the fall—is Jesus.

There are times when we face adversity that it is too great to go to friends or family for help. Things seem so desolate that our hearts long for the One who created us. All roads lead back to Jesus Christ and His power.

The fall builds faith. When we are in the pit and struggle to think of a way out, Jesus proves Himself to be the Almighty. There are things that happen in life that only God can handle—hurdles that we can't overcome without Him interceding for us.

And when the Good Shepherd does step in, we get to see His glory for what it is. We get to see that the hand that holds us can do all things, including saving us from the fall.

If anything, we should count it all as joy to experience the fall and have Jesus come to our rescue. James provides a beautiful scripture to reflect on when we fall to keep in perspective that we will rise again (***The Holy Bible, New International Version,* 2011/1973, James 1:2–4**):

> Consider it pure joy, my brothers and sisters, whenever you face trials of many kinds, because you know that the testing of your faith produces perseverance. Let perseverance finish its work so that you may be mature and complete, not lacking anything.

Don't count yourself out when you fall multiple times. Sometimes, you may find yourself drifting in and out of closeness with God—but never quit drawing close to Him.

As long as you keep returning and repenting, there's still a chance of a relationship with the Good Shepherd. God is not looking for perfection. So keep trying, and if you fall, remember that your faith is being refined in the process.

It's better to follow the Good Shepherd or keep walking in faith than do nothing and go nowhere. Each time you fall, God's plan remains unaffected. He will use you for great things, no matter how often you fall. Multiple offenses do not disqualify you from coming to church, seeking a relationship with Jesus, and repenting many more times.

Falling Is Not Failure, It's a Chance for Forgiveness

We can call out to Him when we fall. Even with trembling voices, afraid of what will happen next, it's better to call out to God rather than brave the fall alone. Think about Peter denying Jesus three times but receiving assured forgiveness. God is gracious that our fall is an opportunity for Him to extend forgiveness and teach us how to do the same.

Also, when Jonah ran, God found him and forgave him by allowing him to fulfill his purpose. God could have easily removed the purpose He had for Jonah as a way to punish him for running, but He chose forgiveness. The Lord uses our fall to gift us reconciliation, peace, grace, and forgiveness in Him.

Sure, we fall, but God is never done working on us. We shouldn't be consumed by the fall, because when we are, it means we are focused on our inequities rather than on the power of God. If we keep our eyes on the Good Shepherd, we stand to receive more, including forgiveness for our sins. The Bible says, "In him we have redemption through his blood, the forgiveness of sins, in accordance with the riches of God's grace" (***The Holy Bible, New International Version,*** **2011/1973, Ephesians** 1:7). Jesus overflows with goodness for us. Even when we aren't faithful, He is—because that's His character.

Take a look at David's story in 2 Samuel 11. David was at his peak. He was a king with a well-established throne, his enemies were defeated, and the nations were preparing to build a temple in Jerusalem (**Newheiser, 2020**). Suddenly, David falls into sin. He steals a man's wife and takes the life of her husband to cover up his sin. The Bible tells us that what David did displeased the Lord (***The Holy Bible, New International Version,*** **2011/1973, 2 Samuel 11**:27).

Yet, when David is confronted by Nathan, a prophet sent by God, he repents in 2 Samuel 12:13. It is his repentance and admission of fault that speaks to God's compassion. God forgives David, but, of course, he still experiences the natural consequence of his fall. Don't be discouraged when you fall. Instead, turn your face to Jesus again. Be someone who doesn't take advantage of His grace but honors it by approaching Him confidently every season. Claim Jesus' forgiveness and grace for yourself daily. It would be foolish to wallow in the ditch that the fall left you in. Rather, be someone who receives the gift of His grace and the forgiveness He offers you.

We don't need to spend our days wallowing in self-pity. If we've fallen, Jesus is our source of freedom and forgiveness. We should get up and move toward Him. We don't need to pay penance when we enter the presence of the Good Shepherd. We only need to be sincere and desperate for the transformation we know He can bring.

Maybe you are having a really tough time in your life, and you believe it's too late for you to climb out of your pit. I'm here to say it's not too late. The message of the Gospel is for everyone, including you. If Jesus were to withhold forgiveness from you, you'd be left with no hope, and that would defeat the purpose of His journey in Gethsemane.

Christ went through everything He did—the captivity, the torture, the crucifixion on the cross, and His resurrection—for you. And Jesus would do it again in a heartbeat.

The Good Shepherd's love for you goes beyond your pit. His love is faithful and will reach in to pull you out—trust Him. Cling to Him. Let Jesus convict your heart to make the most of your days. Christ wants His relationship with you to be a priority above all other things. He wants you to follow Him closely, so He will always extend forgiveness for your shortcomings. Don't let the fall convince you that you've failed too much for God's grace to reach you.

Falling Is Not Failure, It's God's Pruning Process

The fall is a pruning process. When God prunes us, it's for our growth. He reminds the disciples that they will all fall in time because they are human—just as you and I are. The question is: Will we remember the Word of the Lord when we fall into a trench that looks too deep to crawl out of? Do we trust God to grow us in challenging moments so that we can become stronger and more faithful than ever before? Falling is only failure if you choose not to get back up.

Also, Jesus wants to see us bear fruit as sheep who follow or return to Him. The Bible tells us that we can genuinely spot Christ's followers by the fruit of the Spirit. If we aren't bearing fruit, it means we have fallen away from Him. Jesus tells us that every person who is in Him continues to bear love, joy, peace, forbearance, kindness, goodness, faithfulness, gentleness, and self-control (***The Holy Bible, New International Version,* 2011/1973, Galatians 5:22–23**). If we bear none of these, we are like dead branches that need to go through a pruning process. Jesus takes away the branches that do not bear fruit; He cuts off and prunes them to be fruitful (***The Holy Bible, New International Version,* 2011/1973, John 15:2**). The pruning process for God is a way to develop us spiritually and grow our faith.

Sometimes, falling happens so God can do what He does best. The entire process will help build our relationship with the Good Shepherd. There are things we do daily that hinder our closeness to Jesus, so He steps in to reveal these things and pull us away from them.

It can be easy to think that God is punishing us for our mistakes, but He isn't. The Good Shepherd wouldn't pay this much attention to us if He didn't love us. Everything He does to prepare and prune us is out of love. Each time we fall, it's an opportunity to trust Jesus with our challenges and hurt. It's important not to give up when we fall. Instead, let's embrace the fall as we inch our way back to Jesus. He will renew us and help us bear fruit in Him once again.

Not If, But When We Fall

The fall is an inevitable part of our flesh. We fall and falter on numerous occasions. We fall into unhelpful habits, thinking patterns, damaging behaviors, and more. Life is not a matter of *if* we fall but *when* we do. Falling can leave us feeling helpless, but take courage because we have a living hope.

Dealing with the fall is difficult, which is why no one wants to experience it. But we are not meant to do it all alone. When we fall, we have a chance to put our trust in God. It's a chance to ask for His help and involve Him in our lives. Of course, don't go out and fall deliberately, but when the inevitable happens, put your faith in Jesus. Like all other times, don't push His presence and help away in those moments. The Good Shepherd wants to pick you up and use the fall to change your life. God will always hold space for you and restore you, just as He did for Peter.

Just as certain as the fall is for us, Jesus' character remains unchanging. We see this example when Jesus restores Peter after his fall and reminds him that He is still the solid rock. Jesus even asks Peter to feed His sheep and follow Him again. It shows how the Good Shepherd's vision and plan for us don't change because we fall. If anything, God uses those moments to draw us close to Him and reveal more to us.

The Fall Reveals Our Need for God

We were created for communion with God. As people made in His image, we fall whenever we defy His direction. Our rebellion against God's Word lands us in a pit. When we are disobedient, we descend into sin, shame, and fall. The fall is part of the creation, fall, and redemption narrative. Creation speaks to what God intended and made. The fall shows what happened to us because of sin. Lastly, redemption tells what God has done and continues to do to help us.

The implications of removing the fall from our journey can be disastrous. For instance, if there's creation and no fall, we can't explain all the bad things that happen in this world. If redemption exists without the fall of creation, it becomes necessary. It is through the fall that we learn who God is and that He is greater than all beings and experiences. Jesus is the hope for new life and leads us toward Heaven and beyond this fallen earth.

When we fall, it reveals our need for God. Falling makes us face our human frailty. The only true hope we have is in Jesus. We are more susceptible to falling, but in His strength, we can rise and do more. As the Apostle Paul says, we can do all things through Christ who strengthens us (***The Holy Bible, New International Version, 2011/1973, Philippians 4:13***). There's nothing we can do on our own strength without getting exhausted, depressed, confused, fearful, and so on. But when we fall and allow God to do in us what He does best, we are in a good position to see our lives become something extraordinary. How good is God to remain our solid foundation and catch us in moments of falling or even restore us after we've fallen?

While God's creation is good, the sin, corruption, and havoc on earth aren't. As God's image bearers, the Good Shepherd becomes our remedy and shield from the chaos we experience today. Jesus covers our shame and shifts the blame for us. He offers us promises of victory over this world's issues. The good news of the Gospel is that, in rescuing us, Jesus gives us the authority in Him to rise from the fall and defeat the enemy. Praise the Lord. We are so grateful to have Him to meet every need we have.

The Fall Teaches Us to Depend on the Good Shepherd

Mark 14:27–31 highlights that there are times when Jesus' sheep fall away, meaning we may find ourselves offended by the Gospel and struggling to trust what Jesus says to us. Some of us are believers who have fallen away from God because of distrust. Maybe we hoped that Jesus would stop something we deem *bad* from happening in our lives, but He didn't, so we lost trust in His process. But others of us are still longing to believe and may be in an awkward period in life where we feel offended by certain things that must change as we follow Him. Either way, no one is exempt from the fall.

When we fall, it shows us that we can rely on Jesus, the Good Shepherd, to restore us. In Him, the fall has no power over us. God's mercies and favor over our lives are new every morning. His compassion for us never fails, even when we fall (***The Holy Bible, International Version,* 2011/1973, Lamentations 3:2**2). That means He doesn't let His pursuit of us tire. His compassion doesn't get stale or grow old, waiting for us to be perfect. The Good Shepherd is fully aware of our imperfections, yet He chooses to love and shepherd us. He never grows tired of helping us up. Jesus' love is far too great, and His compassion is far too consistent not to be made new every morning! Jesus accounts for our recurring mistakes. Let us get into the habit of relying on Him daily.

Much like the Good Shepherd told Peter, He also warns us that we will fall away (***The Holy Bible, New International Version,* 2011/1973, Mark 14:27**). We should depend on Jesus because He predicts the fall and also has a solution for it. All the resources we need to rise from the fall and survive it are found in Him. We should stick closely to the Good Shepherd, and He will lead us along the right path as we navigate the terrain of fallen sheep. None of us are immune to difficulties or exempt from the fall. If anything, hardships teach us to depend on the Good Shepherd who knows what's ahead and can protect us when the time comes.

Every single one of us needs the Good Shepherd to help us when we begin to fall away. There's no pointing fingers at who needs Him more. We all need Jesus because His presence in our lives is the only saving grace from sin and the consequences of falling.

The Good Shepherd Responds When We Fall

We make mistakes, mess up, and blow it; we will fall many times in life. Pastors, leaders, business owners, parents—you name it, we all fall. Every time we wander or view our problems as bigger than God's promises, we fall. But the grace of God is ready to respond to us.

The Good Shepherd doesn't sit on the sidelines when we fall. He acts to bring us back to Him. Let's read biblical proof of this in Jesus' response to the disciples (***The Holy Bible, New International Version,* 2011/1973, Matthew 12:11–12**):

> He said to them, "If any of you has a sheep and it falls into a pit on the Sabbath, will you not take hold of it and lift it out? How much more valuable is a person than a sheep!"

Jesus' response when we fall is to extend His hand to us. He yearns to rescue and recover us. I don't know what pit you've fallen into, but God will pull you out of it. Nothing can overcome Him, and nothing is too shameful for Him to save you from.

When we fall, the Good Shepherd responds with compassion. He doesn't scold or belittle us. He doesn't turn away from us. Instead, He lovingly offers His grace and restores us to life again (*The Holy Bible, New International Version,* **2011/1973, Psalm 71:19–20**). If you are in a pit, let God help you. Go to Him, be born again by being baptized in water and the Holy Spirit (*The Holy Bible, New International Version,* **2011/1973, John 3:5**). Accept Jesus into your life to embrace His response to you.

Letting Jesus rescue us takes away a lot of stress. Being the Good Shepherd that He is, Jesus has a hook at the tip of His staff and responds to our falling by lifting us out of the pit. Only Jesus Christ can pull us away from the edge that we're about to fall over. With the Good Shepherd watching us, we don't have to fear falling. He provides grace and security. Jesus keeps us from staying permanently trapped in the pit.

Jesus Lifts Us Up and Out

I won't say, "Falling doesn't matter," because it does. Falling changes something in us, and it ushers in experiences that might otherwise have been avoidable. But Jesus comes to our rescue. Yes, you read that correctly—our turning point when we fall is Jesus. He steps in and makes our experiences new again.

Jesus doesn't forsake us. Instead, He lifts us up and out of situations that we find ourselves in. Sometimes, we create our own traps and lie in them—for example, being distracted by worldly attitudes. One of the biggest traps we set for ourselves—and tend to fall into in this world—is comparison and the desire for more possessions. We want more and more things that make us look happy or fulfilled in life, and in doing so, we fall into the trap of endlessly chasing them.

We chase jobs, cars, houses, status, and other things. Yet, we make excuses when it comes to following Jesus: *I'm too busy*, *I forgot*, or *I didn't have time*. These thoughts can overwhelm our minds until we fall into a cycle where joy and fulfillment seem out of reach. We can so easily believe that life's trials and difficulties are all there is to our journey. We forget that Jesus is there to lift us up and out!

This mindset can keep us stuck in a motion that pulls us further into the hole or situation we are facing. But everything shifts when we refocus our eyes on Jesus.

Remember that at the bottom of anything, there's a rock. In this case, the rock at the bottom of what seems like a hard situation is the Lord. He is ready to pull us up. All we need to do is trust His holy hands. Jesus is there to catch us when we are disappointed by things we thought would satisfy us. He is there when we've run out of breath chasing materialism. Jesus steps in when we are worn out and feel abandoned by the very world that deceives us. He steps in and reminds us that He loves us, knowing we are prone to stray, sleep, and fall.

In our fallen place, Jesus' Word tells us the same as He did the disciples: "Come, follow me" (***The Holy Bible, New International Version,*** **2011/1973, Matthew 4:19**). He still wants us and longs for a personal connection with each of us. If this doesn't encourage us, maybe we are stuck in our minds and not reflecting on it deeply enough with our hearts.

Shepherds pull their sheep up and out of trenches when they fall in, and the Good Shepherd's nature is to save us. He came on earth to die for our sins, so don't be afraid to call on Him when you fall. He'll rescue you every time.

You might not even know where you are, but God always will. He won't be waiting for your GPS coordinates when you call on Him; He's right there, close by—just call on Him. You may not feel worthy, but the good news doesn't depend on your feelings; it is realized through the essence of God. So let Him do what a Good Shepherd does and take over. You won't regret letting Jesus lift you up.

Jesus does not need us to reach out to Him for His work to be done in us. But let's get into a habit of stretching our arms to Him because our reach is a sign of faith. For the Holy Spirit to move in our lives, He needs a heart posture that's surrendered to Him. Reaching for Him always helps. Maybe you are thinking to yourself, "God, why do I have to reach? What if I don't have the strength to?" I've been there. The good news is that Jesus enters the mess with us. Remember, the Good Shepherd goes ahead of us.

He knew you'd fall in the trench before it happened, so He already has a solution for your fall. Be encouraged. The Gospel is clear: We are found, even when we stray, run, or fall. There's no need Jesus can't meet, no pain He can't heal, and no sadness He can't turn into joy. Your situation may not change, but Jesus will always transform your heart about the situation when you turn to Him. God is just that good.

In the face of what seems like a hopeless situation, Jesus steps in for us. He steps in for *you*. In the midst of anxiety, shame, and regret, don't turn away from God's presence—call out to Him. Pray in moments of destruction when it feels like you are sinking deeper into the rut. Pray until the Good Shepherd intervenes. One thing you can trust is that He will not ignore your call. When we believe in the Good Shepherd or have hearts longing to know Him, He hears our cries and lifts us up from trouble (***The Holy Bible, New International Version, 2011/1973, Psalm 34:1***7). He is closer to each of us than our very breath. So, reach for Jesus when you fall; He will grab your hand and pull you out.

Chapter 8:

Jesus' Sheep—Found

Anyone who is found was lost to begin with. Being lost can be described as going astray, experiencing defeat, being destroyed, and living in a state of hopelessness (***Once We Were Lost: What It Means to Be Found in Christ,*** **n.d.**). That's how we are when we attempt to live outside of the Creator of life.

Matthew 18:10–14 contains a parable Jesus shares of a man who owns a hundred sheep. This man cares for his sheep so much that if one strays and gets lost, he leaves the majority to find the one—and is overjoyed when he does (***The Holy Bible, New International Version,*** **2011/1973, Matthew 18:12–1**3). Jesus says that, in the same way, He is happier about finding the one lost sheep than about the ninety-nine that have been safe with Him all along (***The Holy Bible, New International Version,*** **2011/1973, Matthew 18:**14). The Good Shepherd cares for us so much that He will leave the majority who are closely following Him in the pen to find the one who is lost. Praise God.

It's quite eye-opening to realize how we can become so complacent and comfortable in our daily lives that we drift away from God's plans for us. The good news is that lost things aren't without purpose; they simply need to be found. Also, we may drift, but it's never too far for Him to find us.

Imagine dashing out of the door in a hurry to jump in your car and fetch your child from school or head somewhere else that's important. You put your hand in your pocket, searching for your car keys, only to find they aren't there. Met with this realization, you'd probably do what anyone else would: dash back into the house to hunt for those keys. See, you wouldn't just shrug and go about your day without finding your keys.

Now, take that very human analogy and apply it to this situation. When we are lost, Jesus doesn't panic or have to search hard. He isn't wondering where we might be. In fact, Jesus doesn't view our being lost as an inconvenience to Him. Instead, He does what a Good Shepherd would do—He finds us exactly where we are.

To Be Found in Jesus Christ

A relationship with Jesus is better than any connection we could think of putting our time and effort into. Paul wrote it best in **Philippians 3:7–9** where he expressed his deep desire to know Him. Everything we value pales in comparison to what Jesus offers. To be found in Jesus introduces the idea of union with the Good Shepherd (**Parnell, 2013**).

To be found in Jesus is to accept His gift and plan for us, while coming to the end of ourselves. When we become found in Jesus, our entire personhood is reshaped and redefined in and through Him. Jesus' suffering on the cross and bloodshed make us alive in Him. Being found in Jesus is for all humanity. Jesus pulls us from a sinful pit and makes us new in Him. We become an entirely new humanity and world as we are reconciled as one body through the cross (*The Holy Bible, New International Version,* **2011/1973, Ephesians 2:14–19**).

Like Paul, who wrote about his desire to know Christ more, forsaking all other things, we need to make the decision to accept being found in Him. We should long to gain Jesus above all worldly treasures. When we allow ourselves to accept being found in Jesus, we experience a depth of faith that makes us right with God—one that is not based on our own works (*The Holy Bible, New International Version,* **2011/1973, Ephesians 2:8–9**).

There's no other source of salvation but Jesus Christ. Being found in Him starts with acceptance and is demonstrated through faith in the fact that He saved us. Jesus is the way, the truth, and the life.

We Are Found in Jesus: Let's Unpack This

Theologically, the world has two divisions: the old age marked by humanity in Adam and the new creation marked by humanity in Christ (***The Holy Bible, New International Version,* 2011/1973, Romans 5:12–21**). We are found in the Good Shepherd because He came to eliminate death, which was guaranteed in the age of Adam, and bring life.

Are you aware that living lost was never what God intended for any of us? Think back to Adam and Eve. God created them to enjoy and care for the Garden of Eden. They were meant to spend their days in relationship with Him. God's intention for us was always Himself—to live in His goodness, abundance, and freedom (**see Genesis** 2).

But the fall came in Genesis 3 when Adam and Eve ate from the only tree in the garden God instructed them not to. That's when greed, disobedience, and the rest of the fallen world came into existence. After going against and hiding from God, Adam and Eve were banished from Eden. In all this turmoil, humanity began to live outside of God's intention, drenched in sin, ungodly desires, and disobedience—all the things that lead to spiritual death.

That was until Jesus. When the Good Shepherd stepped in, He did so as a second chance. Before Jesus gifted us grace, we were on a destructive road with no way out. Redemption was far beyond our reach. Then, Jesus found us and called us back to Him. Now, instead of instant destruction, we have a choice. In finding us, Jesus urges us to choose life in Him (***The Holy Bible, New International Version,* 2011/1973, Deuteronomy 30:19**). Our families can also come to know Jesus by seeing His love beaming in us.

We are found in Jesus because He extends His grace beyond any lawful punishment we deserve. Jesus comes into our lives with the gift of grace, for none of us could ever pay the price for our sin. He stepped in and covered the cost. Jesus Christ came with the gift of grace that shows no favorites and overflows to us all. When our judgment as humanity in the old age was rooted in condemnation, Jesus found us and wiped the slate clean. He offered us the gift of grace, which replaced condemnation with justification. Of course, since we live in a fallen world, we will face trouble. Being found in Jesus doesn't exempt us from difficulties. If anything, walking with the Good Shepherd is a wild journey. We are constantly called to put our faith into action by stepping out of our comfort zones and into what God wants for us. Think of Peter when he was found in Jesus. He was in a boat but was called out of safety onto the waves (*The Holy Bible, New International Version,* 2011/1973, Matthew 14:28–29). When Jesus calls us into discomfort, we have to fix our eyes on Him and trust that He won't let us sink.

Being found in Jesus is allowing Him to do extraordinary things with our ordinary lives. There's an undeniable blessing in being renewed by the Holy Spirit and walking where Jesus calls us. We are found in Jesus, which means we have the joy of seeing lost sheep rescued and our lives turned around by Him. We are no longer lost, but free to live in a world of trouble without crippling anxiety, shame, or worry. Being found in Christ is a hope that reminds us nothing can separate us from Jesus' love.

Jesus wants you. That's why He will leave the majority to find you (*The Holy Bible, New International Version,* 2011/1973, Matthew 18:12–14). He is not willing to let any of His flock go. To be found in Him conveys a deep union and oneness with God. We are made in His image and chosen by Him—being found in Jesus is huge. We receive the title of "righteous" through the justification process when we should still be wearing the title of "sinner." Being found in Jesus changes everything for us!

The Good Shepherd Is Personal

When Jesus said, "I am the Good Shepherd," things became very personal for us (*The Holy Bible, New International Version,* 2011/1973, John 10:11). This revelation of truth is Jesus telling us how much He cares for us—enough to lead us as His sheep. The Good Shepherd loves us and truly wants to relate deeply with us.

God created us, knowing that we are dependent beings. We were created with a need for a personal relationship with Jesus. We were never meant to be independent of Him or of the flock. Jesus has compassion for each of us and encourages us to lean in His direction.

The parable of the lost sheep is proof of how personal Jesus is. He looks for one sheep that has wandered because He cares for it personally. Jesus' love for us is intentional. He doesn't say, "Oh well, there goes so-and-so wandering again. I'll leave that sheep to do its own thing." Jesus knows the dangers of the world, so when we're lost, He searches and brings us back home to Him.

Life can get tricky. It can leave us feeling overwhelmed and questioning our self-worth—until we allow ourselves to get personal with our Lord and Savior, Jesus Christ. When we are found in Him, life's challenges may stay the same, but our hope in the Lord grows stronger. We begin to see things as God intended, and His will becomes visible to us on earth as He declared it in Heaven (*The Holy Bible, New International Version,* 2011/1973, Matthew 6:10).

In **Matthew 18:12–14**, Jesus reminds us that He has created us all with value. Even those who wander and get lost are found in His love. Jesus' relationship with us is personal; He wants to have an intimate connection with us, so He doesn't let us suffer on our own but finds us and brings us to safety.

A Closer Look Into Intimacy With the Good Shepherd

A personal relationship with Jesus involves an intimate connection with Him, marked by faith, trust, submission, obedience, and closeness. We can establish this intimate connection with Jesus through prayer, worship, and by reading the Bible. Biblical teachings guide our thoughts and behaviors, and when we know come to know Jesus personally, we are changed for the better.

Connection to Jesus goes beyond knowing about and believing in Him. It actually involves welcoming Him into your daily experiences and decisions. This intimacy means checking with Him first before doing anything in your life. Allow Jesus to fulfill His purpose and vision for you. Let Him be a friend in your life—that's what it truly means to be found by Him. Befriending the Good Shepherd is transformative. His love touches and changes every aspect of our being. It is a communion that nourishes us from within. Christ wants us all safe in the pen, so He does what the Good Shepherd does and finds us. Each of us is a priority to Him.

A personal relationship with Jesus is about consistency. Constantly choose to return and repent regularly. Jesus' arms are always wide open to receive us. When we are found, our mistakes and shortcomings aren't held against us. We are wiped clean and offered a new start. Being intimate with Jesus also involves vulnerability. Sure, Jesus already knows what you need and what's in your heart, but He enjoys it when you tell Him, anyway. That's what being found in Him is about.

You get to share what's in your heart and serve Him for all your days. Better is one day spent with Jesus than a thousand outside of the pen. Truth is also at the center of your relationship with Jesus. He wants you to come with an open and nondefensive heart; bring Him all your mess because He isn't afraid of it. The relationship only works if you want it to. The Good Shepherd will not pressure you to seek His counsel, but He is always there when you are honest about your needs.

When we are connected to Jesus, the focus will always shift from our actions to the actions of the Good Shepherd. He always finds us, both inside and outside of the pen. We are all God's priceless possessions, which means He deeply treasures us. When you realize that you are number one to God, no matter how your past looks, it changes you. It changes your heart.

A Promise of Eternal Life

Sometimes, we get so caught up with work schedules, family responsibilities, and taking care of ourselves that we lose sight of eternal life. Eternal life with Jesus starts with how we live today. When our life on earth ends, it isn't the final ending. Those who establish a genuine and lasting relationship with God on earth will enjoy eternal life with Him in Heaven. What we focus on today matters because time goes quickly, and the Bible tells us that this life is nothing more than a passing vapor compared to eternity in Heaven. Jesus is the most equipped shepherd we could ever have. All of creation is in the palm of His hand, and He knows every detail about us. When we are found in Jesus, our eyes are open to the path He paved for us to enter the promise of eternal life with Him—the best pasture of all.

Eternal life comes through knowing Jesus intimately and accepting all He has done for us. People who refuse Him basically give themselves over to the punishment that Jesus came to take away. The Bible shares a story of an expert in the law who was curious about the requirements to inherit eternal life (***The Holy Bible, New International Version, 2011/1973, Luke 10:25***). In response to his curiosity, Jesus asks him to reflect on God's Word and the commands of the Law. In doing so, the person realizes that to inherit eternal life, he must love.

Luke 10:27 reminds us that we should love God with all our hearts, souls, strengths, and minds, and love our neighbor as ourselves. (***The Holy Bible, New International Version, 2011/1973, Luke 10:27***). This means intimacy with the Lord must be our priority, just as intimacy with us is His priority.

We should focus on a relationship with Jesus, being found in Him, over and above all the blessings that come from it. Our objective on this earth should be to love God and extend His love to people in radical ways. In a world full of judgment and hate, we need to be examples of love as Jesus has been to us. When we are close to the Good Shepherd and in fellowship with Him, the promise of eternal life is set in motion for us (***The Holy Bible, New International Version, 2011/1973, 1 John 2:25***).

We love by letting go of all else to follow Jesus intimately. When we start, we love by returning to Him daily. When we fall, we love by calling on Him to pull us out of the pit. When we sleep, we love by reconnecting with His Word and principles. Essentially, it's good for us to stick with Jesus and run the race of faith. Jesus has created and opened the door for us to step into everlasting life with Him. But as the Good Shepherd, He will never force us to be with Him. Instead, we are constantly reminded that we are found as His sons and daughters, and we are invited into communion with Him. It's like when we stray as sheep—the pen gate is always open for us to return. However, the Good Shepherd won't forcibly pick us up from where we are; we need to let Him in. The promise of eternal life is simply a byproduct of His unfailing love for us.

Now that you're aware, you should start critically thinking about where you are in your walk with the Good Shepherd. Are you following closely within the pen? Have you strayed? Are you asleep, ready to be woken up? Have you fallen? Are you running? Do you know that you are found in Christ? I hope you can take an honest look at your proximity and make the decision to submit yourself to the loving arms of Jesus.

You Need to Make a Decision to Let the Good Shepherd Into Your Heart

If you've drifted away, run back. If you're sleeping, wake up. If you've fallen, reach for His hand. Turn away from your old ways because they aren't working. If you are honest with yourself, you know they haven't been working for a while now. This is the chance for you to make a decision to let the Good Shepherd in. Let Jesus guide you on how to follow Him. Let Him soften your heart so you can receive all His goodness and everything else He has prepared for you.

Jesus is always there, waiting for you to accept Him into your heart and life. To be found in Him, you must make the decision to trust Him, even just a little. The Bible says that faith as small as a mustard seed can move mountains (***The Holy Bible, New International Version, 2011/1973,* Matthew 17:20–21**). All you need to do is show up, believe in the goodness of Jesus, and be willing to develop a relationship with Him. Jesus will do all the heavy lifting. As His people and sheep, all we are called to do is to decide. Jesus presents us with the option of eternal life with and in Him or the alternative that leads to death (**read Deuteronomy 30:**19). We stand to gain much more when we choose Jesus, lean on Him, and let Him into our experiences.

He takes care of the rest. Deciding to let Jesus in reminds me of the sweet hymn *Amazing Grace* by John Newton (1725–1807). It assures us of joy and salvation in Christ. Being found in Jesus is like a warm blanket of love that wraps around us, providing comfort, just as we find solace in this song (***Amazing Grace,*** **n.**d.):

> Amazing grace! how sweet the sound,
>
> That saved a wretch; like me!
>
> I once was lost, but now am found,
>
> Was blind, but now I see.
>
> 'Twas grace that taught my heart to fear,
>
> And grace my fears relieved;
>
> How precious did that grace appear
>
> The hour I first believed!
>
> The Lord hath promised good to me,
>
> His word my hope secures;
>
> He will my shield and portion be
>
> As long as life endures.
>
> When we've been there ten thousand years,
>
> Bright shining as the sun,
>
> We've no less days to sing God's praise
>
> Than when we first begun.

These words describe our lives. When we step out of our own way and allow the Good Shepherd to redeem and love us, things change. There's nothing we can do for ourselves that could ever compare to what Jesus does for us. It is by His amazing grace that we are found in Christ. He lifts us from the wreckage of sin and makes us right. When we are found in Christ, He rescues us from destruction and shields us from our own destructive behaviors. May the hymn *Amazing Grace* remind you of the fullness that comes with making the decision to follow Jesus.

Decide to Turn to the Good Shepherd

Making the decision to turn to Christ and be found in Him relieves fear, revives hope, and restores goodness in our lives. Let the grace of God hold you, even in your messiest moments. You are never too far gone for Christ's love to touch and change you. Your habits are not too stubborn for the Good Shepherd. You'll never regret making Jesus the center of your world.

The gate that leads to eternal life with Jesus is narrow, while the one that involves pleasing the world is broad and leads to destruction (***The Holy Bible, New International Version,* 2011/1973, Matthew 7:13**).

The road to spend eternity with the Good Shepherd begins now, and it is a narrow one, but there is room for you. The world has become comfortable choosing trends and wayward culture over God's Word. However, that doesn't have to be your story.

We live in a time when people are lukewarm toward the things of God's kingdom or disinterested in following Jesus. We think we have time to laze around and don't take salvation seriously. But Jesus is coming back for us. And it is up to us to decide what state we will be in when He returns. Will He find us ready, already following Him closely? Or will He find us wandering, walking away from the eternal life He offers?

Each of us has the option to turn to the Good Shepherd today. We do not have the luxury to sit back and be on the fence about choosing Jesus any longer. Don't allow your faith to be watered down by the fleeting pleasures of this world. Decide to put your faith in Jesus and keep turning to Him, as He must be your source to sustain life.

Decide to Surrender to the Good Shepherd

Make the decision to surrender your will to God's plan and purpose for you. As human beings, we tend to live under this belief that we have complete control over our lives, but in reality, we don't. The Good Shepherd has complete control. When we entertain false beliefs, we eventually begin to see them as truth, and that's when frustration comes into play. Being found in Christ is about letting go of that idea of control. Let the Good Shepherd, who truly is in control, take the lead in every situation in your life.

Our choices really affect what happens in our lives. When we try to keep control instead of giving it to Jesus, we tend to make poor choices, and our lives fill up with endless worry. That's until the Good Shepherd finds us and gives us a different option—surrender.

Jesus wants us to decide to put faith in Him above the belief that we can do things on our own. That's what surrender is. There's beauty in relinquishing the need to control how our lives pan out and trusting Jesus to work it out.

Surrender is not the same as quitting, especially when you leave your life in the hands of the One who made it (**Ward, n.d.**). Deciding to surrender means giving into God's control. It's about leaning into His sovereignty. When we choose to surrender, we make Holy Spirit-led choices that often influence the outcome positively.

Many times, we confuse courage and strength with being in control. Yet, the bravest thing we can do for ourselves is to relinquish control and approach life with faith. Of course, do your part, and do whatever God leads you to do. Let God do the rest.

Decide to Trust the Good Shepherd

The decision to surrender involves trusting God's nature and intentions above what you currently see. For example, if you feel lost, keep walking in faith alongside Jesus and trust that He is aligning your steps and bringing you to a place of feeling found.

Being found in Christ makes us feel completely safe. When we put our faith in Him, we are secure in who we are and trust in His provision. In a world where relationships feel like revolving doors, with people continuously coming and going, it can be hard to trust.

Sometimes, when trust is broken in our lives, we tend to project that distrust onto our relationship with God. Yet, His presence offers us emotional safety. Jesus will not change on us.

Feeling safe is to be seen, heard, known, and loved—all of which are found in Christ alone. **Proverbs 29:5** clearly states that anyone who trusts in Jesus is safe. He is our refuge, confidence, hope, and security.

We are protected when we lean on His name because it is "a fortified tower" where we can hide and be safe (*The Holy Bible, New International Version,* **2011/1973, Proverbs 18:10**). Going back to the parable of the lost son, when we returned home, he wanted to be found and kept safe in his father's yard. And when he arrived, he was embraced beyond what he could have imagined. Jesus opens His arms to us in the same way.

Decide to Declare the Good Shepherd's Name—Jesus Christ

The Bible says, if we confess with our mouths, believe that Jesus died and rose again for our sins, and make Him Lord over our hearts, we will be saved (*The Holy Bible, New International Version,* **2011/1973, Romans 10:9–10**). Your heart changes when you accept and declare Jesus as your Lord and Savior—when you see Him as the one and only Good Shepherd.

Also, trusting God means recognizing that we are incapable without Jesus. In life, we've become accustomed to the concept of self-sufficiency. People claim to be self-made, but the truth is, no one truly is. We were all created by God with a specific purpose. Whenever we feel tempted to rely on "self," we buy into the lie that we can live without Him.

Decide to Approach Life With Truth and Compassion

Being found in Jesus means removing the lies from our lives and approaching life with truth. It's knowing that things won't end well if we try to do them without Jesus. He is our best and only option to succeed and walk in purpose, and He's not willing to let us stay lost.

When we are found in Jesus, it becomes easier to extend compassion and grace to others because we know how it feels to be at a turning point in our lives. Jesus offers us grace so we may extend that to people inside and outside the pen. Paul tells us to be "full of grace" when we speak to others **(*The Holy Bible, New International Version,* 2011/1973, Colossians 4:6).** We can only receive this fullness of grace from the One who gives it in abundance—Jesus. So when we are found in Him, we are in a better position to extend grace to others.

Being full of grace is hard when we do it without Jesus. But in Christ, we receive this wisdom, and He gives us the right words to say. This helps us become part of the healing in the world. With Jesus, we become better and constantly seek to do better. We may not always get it right, but He walks in step with us, empowering and redeeming us along the way. Jesus is the answer to every question and the comforter of every heart in need. By choosing to be in Him, we turn our gaze toward living in His amazing grace.

Decide to Embrace the Good Shepherd's Gift of Grace and Freedom

Contrary to what the world thinks, it is freeing to be found in Christ. The world wants us to think that choosing Jesus is settling for a life of boredom, but that's not true. When we decide to follow Jesus and are found in Him, it leads to ultimate freedom. This decision actually gives us life. Jesus offers us clarity and peace. Situations may be challenging, as life tends to be, but with Jesus, everything becomes manageable.

Most importantly, make the decision to choose God because He has already chosen you. His love for you isn't going anywhere, so you don't ever have to worry about Him walking away or abandoning you once you've chosen Him. This is the best decision you could make for yourself. God is generous and never short of second chances.

Being found in God means receiving love in a world filled with hatred. It equips you to turn away from worldly pressures and be rooted in things of true value. Being found in Christ empowers you to resist sin and temptation in ways that you couldn't or wouldn't have before. It's just a better life overall. God is worth the decision.

God's love opens doors for acceptance and belonging in a world that often shuns people. Jesus wants to guide us, and His direction is a part of being found in Him. When you make the decision to choose God, He guides you in truth and strengthens you.

Stay Connected

People who are found in God are like branches connected to the vine of life (*The Holy Bible, New International Version,* **2011/1973, John 15:5**). Making the decision to stay connected to Jesus enables us to bear spiritual fruit, such as peace, gentleness, self-control, faithfulness, and kindness. However, without Jesus, we can do nothing. So, when you make the decision to walk with Jesus, keep this scripture in mind.

We receive lasting joy by obeying God's will and staying connected to Him. It's a joy that isn't affected by situations and circumstances. His love leaves us far better than it finds us. The power of being found in Christ is that He changes us in the most gentle and loving way. He affirms us and lifts us out of the wickedness and darkness of this world. Being found in Christ helps us navigate life with a kingdom mindset, enabling us to add value to others' lives. It also sets us apart from the path of this fallen world and helps us become true reflections of life, love, and goodness.

If you are experiencing difficulties right now, call Jesus, who will rescue you. Being found in Christ means you are not a slave of the world anymore.

You hold a new position of authority against principalities and powers. God is working in you, and He is not finished—if only you'll trust Him. As Jesus' sheep who follow, stray, sleep, run, fall, and are found, we need support to continue our faith walk in the pen, and we must draw near to His gates whenever we stray or run outside of it.

Chapter 9:

Daily Living—Walking With the Shepherd

When we walk with God authentically and intimately, we are bound to live purposefully. Walking with the Shepherd is the best thing we can do for ourselves. Living daily in Christ's presence doesn't mean life becomes perfect, but it indicates that we stay connected to the perfector of our faith.

Of course, we all have days when we don't feel as spiritually attuned as we'd like. Sometimes we may feel distant, tired, discouraged, and all other human emotions. But walking with God daily ensures that we are held in His mighty, capable hand—even when life is hard.

No number of off days or feeling distant can change God's love for you. The question is: Do you long to be as near to Him as He does to be with you? Like any relationship, you need to put time and effort into building closeness with the Good Shepherd. You need to invest time, care, and attention into getting to know Him deeply.

Imagine being a spouse who pays no attention to your partner's needs or is disinterested in who they are. That's a recipe for an unhappy union. Similarly, spending your days without prioritizing time with Jesus will result in dissatisfaction.

For your faith to remain active and your belief in Jesus to grow, you need to draw near to Him daily. You may stray, sleep, or fall, but you can always choose to follow Him. You are found in Him, and walking with Jesus is a daily decision.

Practical Ways to Follow the Shepherd

When you care deeply about someone or something, you make time for it. For example, you care about your dental hygiene, so you brush your teeth daily, and some even floss. You care about your family, so you spend uninterrupted time with them after work. The same action is required when approaching God. You can, and should, incorporate practical ways of following Jesus into your daily routine.

Start and End Each Day in Prayer

Spending time with God is about communicating with Him daily. You wouldn't spend an entire day ignoring your spouse; doing that would just be rude, so why do it to Jesus? Prayer is your opportunity to engage with God in conversation. He speaks to you daily, so respond to Him. Get to know what He requires from you and share your thoughts with Him.

Prayer has a way of strengthening faith. It gives us confidence to keep approaching God with our needs and thanksgiving. When we pray, we remain rooted in God's provision and stay connected to the vine. As we keep approaching God in prayer, we develop closeness with Him.

Start and end each day in prayer. Prioritizing prayer establishes closeness with the Good Shepherd. You get to know and hear His voice more often. When God is your first and last point of communication daily, you make headway in many areas of life. That's why we are encouraged to "pray continually" (*The Holy Bible, New International Version,* **1973/2011, 1 Thessalonians 5:17**).

Instead of reaching for your phone, pray in the early morning as soon as you wake up. This encourages a fresh anointing as you start your day in God's presence. Then, when you lie down to sleep at the end of your day, make your last conversation with Jesus so that He is on your mind as you sleep. Continuous and consistent prayer keeps Jesus at the center of all you do.

Choose Your Company Wisely

There are people in life who will make the journey more stressful. Some may point you toward faith, while others delight in misery and will lead you to fear. The truth is, who you surround yourself with matters. The people who speak into your life matter! Do your people point you to faith, saying, "Look at what God is doing through this" during hard times? Or are you hanging around people who discourage you and distract you from God's promises? Your answer to this is important because it also determines how motivated you'll be to prioritize your time with God daily.

Choose your company wisely. The Bible is clear that "bad company corrupts good character" (**The Holy Bible, New International Version, 1973/2011, 1 Corinthians 15**:33). As Jesus' sheep, we must be careful about who we hang around with. We can interact with all people, but not everyone should be in our close circle of advisors. For example, Jesus was accessible to anyone who needed and called on His name, but He only shared His plans and mission with the 12 disciples. He also chose to walk and minister with those 12 apostles. Have your small circle that can speak faith into your life.

Create Spiritual Boundaries

Think of how a parent sets rules for their children to protect them from getting burned or doing something that can destroy their lives—spiritual boundaries are similar to those rules for us. Christ came so you may have freedom, and setting spiritual boundaries that are informed by biblical principles is a way for you to live freely. You must go above and beyond to shield your heart from falling for the enemy's schemes.

The Bible urges us to be alert because the enemy is looking to devour us, especially when we are off guard (**The Holy Bible, New International Version, 2011/1973, 1 Peter 5:8**). Spiritual boundaries protect us from entertaining things that lead us into temptation and pull us away from the pen. When we are honest with ourselves about the areas where we are weaker or easily give in to the enemy, we can place them at God's feet. Spiritual boundaries are firm parameters we set to keep ourselves from going outside of what God desires for us. Our salvation must be at the forefront of our choices. We need to say no to certain things if we want to follow Jesus. Spiritual boundaries protect us from the contamination of the world. We are safer within the pen and away from the temptation when our boundaries are intact. The Bible instructs that you should "watch your life and doctrine closely" (***The Holy Bible, New International Version,* 1973/2011, 1 Timothy 4:16**). Boundaries save us from things we shouldn't entertain or allow to distract us from Jesus.

Submission or Surrender

Today's self-love and self-reliance culture makes us believe we stand alone. However, walking with God is an act of daily surrender. It shows our willingness to let the One who holds it all lead us because, as people, we don't know more than He does. Surrender is letting go of how we think things should be to embrace Jesus' purpose for us.

Submission involves recognizing that we have been crucified with Christ, so our bodies are no longer our own (***The Holy Bible, New International Version,* 2011/1973, Galatians 2:20**). We live by faith in Him. We forfeit our plan to make room for God's transformative power in our lives as He protects us from the enemy. God sees the bigger picture, and as long as we acknowledge His sovereignty, we will obey Him.

When we stand on God's promises, we are in a better position to surrender to Him. The Bible is a solid foundation for us to take small steps of faith. God's Word is full of beautiful assurances based on His unfailing love and consistent character. Surrendering ourselves to Him helps guard and defend the precious gifts and promises God has entrusted to us. The more we give ourselves over to Him every day, the greater our faith will be in what God can do.

The world wants us to believe in things that are outside of God's will. However, submission and surrender are acts of humility that recognize our need for Jesus and the church. People need one another, which is why Jesus honors fellowship. But most of all, we need Jesus. When we submit ourselves to loving God first and then His people, we fulfill two great commandments, and we also live our daily lives in surrender—obeying God's requests.

Analyze Your Choices and Repent When You've Fallen Short

Are the decisions you are making representing your trust in Jesus, or are you wondering about doing your own thing because the world says so? If you are a believer, you are probably someone's favorite Christian (**Bethesda Senior Living, 2022**). This means someone out there is watching your lifestyle. They will either seek to know God because of how they see you live or be drawn further away from Him. So your choices matter.

If you are someone seeking Jesus, you want to see Him represented in those who already claim to be walking with Him—understandably so. But your own choices to get to know Jesus are also important. Rather than basing your decision to follow Him solely on how other imperfect Christians are doing it, base it on your personal encounter with Him.

Build a relationship with Jesus that you can be proud of, one that's not influenced by how others walk with Him. Purchase a Bible and go outside each day, asking to have an encounter with Jesus until He responds. Your choice to seek the Lord for yourself is a responsibility that you can't put on someone else. Your decisions matter.

We follow the Good Shepherd better when we are focused on Him. So, we should live each day with a sense of urgency to get to know Jesus more deeply. Live a life of service to Him by loving others and seeing ourselves how He does.

Repentance also helps us stay close to Christ and make decisions that reflect our love for Him. In **Acts 26:20**, we are told to repent, turn to God, and show our repentant hearts through our actions. So, our choices matter as we follow or seek to follow Christ. Even when we have repented, sometimes we may slip again and sin. Though God does not desire for us to fall into sin again, it's okay to repent again. Just keep getting back up.

How to Rejoin the Flock After Straying

Walking closely with Jesus is key to staying in communion with Him. However, life can happen and create situations where we drift from this connection. Having a community of people to encourage you back to your faith is important, especially in tough seasons. We are always in danger of straying. The enemy waits for moments when we fall away from God to pick us off one at a time. Sometimes, the enemy will divide us so he can easily get to each of us. Community is a threat to evil plans. We are strengthened when we gather with fellow believers or people who can support us in seeking God's grace. By God's grace, we are shielded when we stay in the flock. Even when we stray, we can always rejoin.

Find Community: Flock Are in Danger When Scattered

Flocks are in danger when scattered. That's why it's important to find community and fellowship with people who are also on a journey with Jesus. Life gets lonely when we attempt to do it on our own. Sheep travel in flocks. In the same way, our friends, mentors, and family are part of our community—they are our flock.

Predators typically circle and enclose sheep when they walk alone. We can easily become prey to the enemy when Jesus isn't at the center of our lives. Both safety and sustenance are found in Jesus and walking alongside other sheep. Our pride and ego will often say, "I don't want to meet with a group of people." They try to convince us that we are self-sufficient.

We can rejoin the flock by valuing the gathering of saints. Finding community isn't just about one flock member, but about all of us. We rejoin the flock through church community, Bible studies with friends, and other activities that allow us to fellowship with others. Rejoining the flock is a way of humbly acknowledging that we need community and that others need us—for accountability, encouragement, and overall spiritual growth.

As the Bible says, we must consider how to encourage one another and gather in support of each other as we see the Lord's Day approaching (*The Holy Bible, New International Version,* **2011/11973, Hebrews 10:24–25**). Living in community with others is living life as God designed it.

When we are in community with one another, we can watch each other's backs and encourage one another to move in God's direction. The journey always seems more manageable when we have people around us enduring together. Our pastors, friends, church family, and others are essential parts of staying close to the Good Shepherd.

Get Close to the Shepherd Through the Bible (SOAP Method)

When you're seeking to rejoin the flock, paying attention to God's Word is imperative. Get close to the Shepherd by reading the Bible and processing it using the SOAP method. SOAP is an approach to Bible study that helps you read the Bible and implement it daily. It stands for scripture, observation, application, and prayer.

First, you start by reading Scripture. When your intention is to seek God, you must listen to what He is saying to you. Reading the Bible is how you can search for genuine peace, connection, and breakthrough. It's the manual you need for life's good times and challenges. Physically write out the scripture so you are repeating it to yourself. It takes discipline to read the Bible and meditate on what God is communicating, so set aside a time to do that daily.

After reading a passage of Scripture several times, observe what's written. Observation takes effort and intentionality. Reading the Bible isn't a "quick fix" option for life's problems. Instead, it's a chance for you to truly understand God's heart. So when you observe His Word, sit in silence and let it work within you. Ask yourself: *How do I interpret the message? Who is the audience? Are there any repetitive words? What stands out to me? Can I find a main theme? What do I believe is the main lesson?* Next is the application. It's not enough just to read God's Word and observe it if you aren't planning to apply it to your life. It's important to live out what you know because that's at the core of your relationship with

Jesus. It may be helpful to reflect on what you believe God is saying to you today based on what you've read. Also, consider how you can apply the lesson to your life and what changes you can make moving forward.

Lastly, pray! Prayer is the final part of the SOAP approach. For God's power to remain active in you, you must let Him in. Prayer opens a door for God to reveal more information to you. Confess to Him how you've interpreted the Word, pray about its application to your life, and ask Him to keep the message alive in your heart. In a world where the Good Shepherd's presence can sometimes feel distant, prayer personalizes God's Word and offers you an opportunity to engage with Him.

You can use the SOAP method daily to help you make the most of your time with God. The more you use this approach to connect with Him, the higher your chances of rejoining the flock when you've strayed. You can also invite your friends or family to use this method with you. This way, each of you can share what you've learned from the Scripture and uplift one another in the process.

Make Time for Jesus in Solitude

Pray that the Lord helps you continue pursuing Him during times of solitude. Many of us can underestimate solitude and silence, but every disciple of Jesus needs to understand its importance. Jesus exemplified the power of solitude in developing intimacy with Him. He continuously withdrew from crowds, responsibilities, life activities, and the demands of ministry to prioritize solitude.

When you spend more time with Jesus, you learn His character and recognize His voice. Remember that only those who know Him and His voice follow more easily. You wouldn't trust a stranger or go where they lead, but you would follow a loved one. Solitude is the chance to make the Good Shepherd your loved one—someone near and dear to you. Be intentional about the time you spend with Him. You'll never lose when you prioritize Jesus. Even when it looks or feels like you are losing, the bond you build with Him will stand as a firm reminder of the good plans

He has for your life (*The Holy Bible, New International Version, 2011/1973, Jeremiah 29:11*). Jesus wants the best for you, and that can only be found when you are close to Him.

Solitude should be used as an ongoing approach to improve your relationship with God. Sure, it may not be perfect, but taking time each day to spend with Jesus will make life more meaningful. You'll start to think more highly about life and the purpose He has given you. Knowing Him more deeply also helps you better understand yourself because you were made in His image. Solitude is also an opportunity to build compassion, wisdom, awareness, and connection with the Good Shepherd. It's a chance to prepare for the trials ahead. In solitude, you allow God to strengthen you and develop wisdom within you for challenging situations.

Jesus prioritized solitude whenever He had to make important decisions. It allowed Him to deal with troubles and emotional turmoil accordingly. We see that image reflected in the scene before His capture in Gethsemane. Jesus left the disciples while they slept to be in solitude and prayer. He invites us to join Him in this practice so we can know God more deeply and share His love with others.

Get back to the basics of spending time with Jesus. Curate a playlist of worship songs and sit in your garden, doing nothing but listening to the praises and the wind. Allow Jesus to touch you in your solitude. Sometimes, I go outside with a notebook and pen and just sit with my eyes closed, saying, "God, speak to me. I'm listening." You can do something similar and have unforced and uninterrupted time with Jesus.

Be Persistent and Patient With Yourself

Faith goes in hand with persistence, patience, and waiting on the Lord. We often think straying is only about nonbelievers. However, many believers start with a fire for Jesus and then become casual Christians along the way. With that in mind, straying is actually about letting our faith become a casual thing. It's about journeying through life, distant from the principles that God has set for us—something that affects both believers and nonbelievers. We demonstrate what it means to pull away from the flock when we aren't persistent, patient, or willing to wait in our relationship with the Good Shepherd. Of course, in a world that wants things and wants them *now*, waiting can feel like punishment. We tend to veer off course when waiting on the Lord because we equate it to the same frustration we may experience when waiting in traffic or for food at a restaurant.

Yet, there's value in waiting, especially when we are waiting on the Good Shepherd. The waiting season is an essential time of preparation for us to encounter more of Jesus. If our hearts are willing to get nearer to Him, we also need to embrace the wait that comes with it.

Also, persist in seeking Jesus. Faith in the Lord is not only about knowing the theology but about constantly opening your heart to Him. Persist in prayer, in worship, in reading your Bible—even when you *don't feel* like it. The profound truth about God's Word is that it will work in you, regardless of your feelings. When you consistently go to Him and keep those lines of communication open, rejoining the flock becomes inevitable because you didn't give up on encountering Him.

The Bible helps us encounter Him. It is written, "The testing of your faith produces perseverance," so don't let the straying keep you from returning to him and rejoining the flock (***The Holy Bible, New International Version,*** **2011/1973, James 1:3**). Consider all the hard times, trials, and temptations as building blocks for your faith.

When you stray, you can easily panic, but don't. Instead, persist and wait on the Lord—He is doing a new thing in you. Jesus' faithfulness is guaranteed, and your faith and endurance to continue making room for Him will be rewarded.

In his letter to the early church, James encourages us to be patient until the Lord returns (***The Holy Bible, New International Version,*** **2011/1973, James 5:7**). This patience is not based on what we can do, but on trusting God with life's ebbs and flows. In the same verse, James points out how a farmer waits patiently through the seasons for the land to yield crops. Farmers demonstrate trust that each season, as it comes and goes, will result in a harvest. You, too, should be patient as you rejoin the flock. Don't condemn yourself for your imperfections; they only show that you need God.

Straying doesn't disqualify you from God's love and desire to redeem you daily, and as long as you keep rejoining the flock, He will use you for great things. The persistence and patience linked to faith are all based on what God does through you. So, even when you rejoin the flock, be cautious not to rely on your own strength. Hand it over to God and let Him anoint, uplift, and strengthen you to walk alongside fellow believers.

Jesus is the only one who can change your heart so that you stray less often. He can use the messiness and challenges you experience to give you a testimony that points back to His goodness. Only trust Him and not imitations. Whatever season you are in at the moment, keep returning to your faithful Shepherd.

Be patient in all seasons of your life, as the farmer demonstrates in the book of James. Turn your face back to God and be patient as you persistently seek to follow Him again. More is accomplished in the heart of patience, compassion, and persistence than could ever be achieved in shame.

Wake Up From Your Sleep

By God's grace, we wake up every morning to a new day. We can be glad and rejoice in that! The sunlight streams into our homes, and we enjoy birds and nature the next day. Some of us set alarm clocks to wake up and start our days off with beautiful music. Others, like myself, have children who welcome the new day with play. The point is that mornings are beautiful and mostly filled with excitement. But the type of sleep you need to be wary of is spiritual.

Spiritual sleep is not as obvious as physical sleep. It isn't marked by birds singing or sunlight streaming through the window. When we are spiritually asleep, it's easy to miss. We may not even be aware that we are sleeping. It's possible to experience life physically awake but fully asleep spiritually. This happens when we aren't seeking God's face daily, or when we let busyness or the day's responsibilities get in the way of our solitude with God.

If we don't intentionally develop our relationship with God, we can easily fall spiritually asleep. We'll notice other things replacing God's time in our lives, and suddenly, we've minimized the meaning of life to our to-do list. There's no greater joy in the day than connecting with the true God, who is alive! Spiritual sleep undermines God's intention for our lives.

Thankfully, we can wake up from sleep. We can rediscover the wonder and miracles of God working in and around us. The key to waking up is reigniting our passion for Jesus and establishing closeness with Him.

Return to Wonder

Wonder is largely attributed to perspective. How we see things affects what we believe. When we encounter wonder, we experience a sense of awe about Jesus, bringing hope to every situation. Life is stressful and busy, but wonder eases that. Wonder helps us refocus and recognize God's presence in our lives. It enables us to step back and witness His glory and movement, noticing signs of His goodness everywhere. What once seemed mundane appears miraculous, and His power becomes more evident through wonder. As a result, we naturally become excited about getting closer to Jesus, making us more spiritually awake.

Go back to when you saw God in everything. If you've never really been that person, start practicing by seeing the good in everything. You are probably spiritually asleep because you've forgotten who God is and how amazingly His hand touches your life daily. Gratitude is a great way to return to your wonder. What can you be grateful for today?

Approach Prayer as a Chance to Talk to God

Talking to God is a spiritual discipline that's meant to motivate us. It's a privilege that shouldn't be taken for granted. When we approach Jesus as if prayer is an obligation, it quickly starts to feel like a chore, and that's not how we approach intimacy with God. Closeness with God through prayer can't happen unless our hearts are fully in it.

We need to devote ourselves to talking to God, staying watchful, and being thankful (*The Holy Bible, New International Version, 2011/1973*, Colossians 4:2). Also, rejoice in the Lord. Instead of focusing on problems and issues in life, turn your focus to what God has given you. Choose to be joyful in His presence and provision.

Prayer is only tedious if you approach it as a prerequisite for Christianity instead of as a joyful conversation with God. Don't let your conversations with the Good Shepherd become ritualistic and empty. Instead, invite wonder into them. Allow yourself to reflect on awe-inspiring moments with Him. Start approaching God with excitement and tell Him about your ideas, dreams, fears, and all the rest once again.

Ask the Holy Spirit for Restoration

The Holy Spirit is your sustenance. Ask Him for what only He can do in you. *Wake me up, Lord* is a simple prayer you can say. Ask for spiritual restoration so you can be alert to the joys and impact of God in your life. Every day, the Good Shepherd gives you chances to learn something new as you draw near to Him. In the process of asking the Holy Spirit to restore your sense of wonder and curiosity about God, you'll find that He inspires spiritual awareness within you.

You can ask the Holy Spirit to restore your spirit and renew your mind. This will help you become more alert. All the things that are barriers to faith or keeping you spiritually asleep are removed through the Holy Spirit. He can work in your spirit and mind to develop spiritual fruit.

The Holy Spirit came to lead and guide us into all truth. This means He will help you stay spiritually awake as He develops your spiritual maturity. The Holy Spirit continually works in our lives to transform us.

Be Proactive, Not Passive

Pursue Jesus daily by reading, talking about Him, traveling, and seeking His wonder. Allow yourself to explore every book of the Bible to learn more about Him. Faith is about being proactive, not passive. Without action, faith is dead (*The Holy Bible, New International Version,* **2011/1973, James 2:17**). You can start small. Find something that interests you about Jesus and let yourself wonder about it. Your curiosity will lead you to search for Him and seek His nature more each day. Do your best to live with an open heart, anticipating what God can do. The more you learn about Jesus, the more you'll feel inspired and notice the beauty around you.

Daily Devotionals to Return After Running Away

Return to God, no matter how far you run or stray. Daily devotionals can be a resource to run back to God after pulling away. You can also use this practice to remain in the pen and grow your faith. Life should be all about spending time with Jesus. Read your Bible, pray, and devote yourself to obeying God's will. Spending regular and intentional time with God is important for your spiritual walk. It fosters an environment for spiritual maturity and deepens intimacy with God.

The Lord yearns to spend time with us and is eager to hear from us daily. Because we are all different, each of us will have a unique relationship with Him. No single devotional habit will work for everyone; you just need to find a routine that works for you. It's helpful to try different ideas and approaches to spending time with God until you find something that feels right. Keep devoting yourself to building your relationship with Him.

Run Back to Jesus

Start wherever you are. If you are a seasoned believer or someone who is still searching, start your return to God slowly. Plan to begin with as little as 10 minutes and gradually increase your time with God. As your level of comfort develops, you'll find yourself staying in devotionals for longer. There are plenty of things you can do to improve your devotional life.

Find a Quiet Place

If you've ever felt spiritually dry or overwhelmed with anxiety, time with Jesus is the remedy. Our souls often long for the Lord, which can manifest as a lack of motivation, a short temper, persistent worry, and a need for belonging. We need Jesus, so every part of us yearns to know Him. Yet, often, we let things get in the way of pursuing Him.

Meet with Jesus in your quiet place, as He demonstrated to His disciples. After a day of ministering, Jesus dismissed the crowd and went to a mountainside to pray by Himself (***The Holy Bible, New International Version,*** **2011/1973, Matthew 14:22–23**). Find a quiet place to connect with Jesus personally. Ideally, it should be a place free from distractions and interruptions. Your quiet place is meant for you to devote yourself to Jesus—a place you can use to praise and honor Him in multiple ways.

For many people, a quiet place with Jesus involves reading the Bible, making creative notes, worshiping, and journaling. To truly get the benefits of salvation, you need to prioritize time with the Lord. Surrender to the transformative work He wants to do in you. Finding a quiet place with Jesus creates an atmosphere to honor Him. In your quiet time with Jesus, He can give you revelations through the Holy Spirit and a peace that surpasses all understanding. Routine quiet time with Jesus is refreshing; it renews and fills us up so we can go into the world as significant contributors.

Worship

Another word for worship is reverence, which means to hold someone in high regard or with great respect and admiration (**Piper, 2016**). When you worship God, you humble yourself before Him and admire His authority. A lot of times, when we think about worship, music comes to mind. That's fitting because music is a part of worship. It allows you to have a channel of expression through which you can pour out your heart to the true and living God. Worship music helps initiate a deep connection with Him.

Create a playlist of worship music that you can learn from. Listening to worship reminds us of how good God truly is. As you worship, move freely around the room and give Jesus your all. Worship can create an environment for you to feel God's presence.

That said, worship isn't just about the songs you sing. Worshiping God is about your lifestyle—learning to value the Kingdom of God above all things. Worship is reflected in your decisions, the words you use, your thoughts, how you respond to the world, and what flows from your heart.

God seeks us to worship Him in spirit and truth (***The Holy Bible, New International Version,* 2011/1973, John 4:24**). This means knowing God's Word and living in obedience to it. It also means only doing things that bring praise to His name.

Read the Bible to Retain and Comprehend

Sometimes, we read the Bible and forget what we've read the second we step away. Lord, help us because we genuinely need the Holy Spirit to soak in God's Word in a way that lasts and impacts our lives. If you, like many others, know how to read the Bible but struggle to remember what you've read and find it difficult to apply it to your life, you are not alone. The mind can wander during the most critical time of the day—Bible reading.

Applying a simple Bible study method can help us read the Bible more efficiently and intentionally. The truth is that to remember God's Word, we need to study it as we would information for a test or examination. Put all your effort into it as though you are going to be tested because you are, though not in a formal, "Take your pens out" kind of way.

To retain biblical information and understand it, you'll need to apply yourself. This means reading and rereading entire passages. Of course, start with one passage or story at a time. Reading passages creatively at least three times, preferably five, can be effective.

We must take a lively approach to Bible reading. Otherwise, it becomes just "another" thing we're doing or feel obligated to do. To keep your reading highly engaging and intentional, you can start by reading an entire passage of your choice as you would normally. Follow this up by rereading the passage aloud and adding character to your voice as if you were reading to a child. Take note of your pitch and inflection as you read.

After the second reading, the third is about picturing yourself in the scene of the passage. Where is it taking place? What smells can you imagine in the air during this time? What do your surroundings look like? What sounds can you hear? Your third reading is all about personalizing the text by putting yourself in the environment.

Next, for your fourth reading, pick a scripture from the larger passage. Reread it and evaluate why it stands out to you. Underline what catches your attention and note the theme you've noticed. Let the words permeate your heart as you pause between reading and truly let the message sink in.

For your fifth reading, jot down any observations that come to mind. What did you realize from putting yourself in the scene? Can you articulate what God is saying to you in the passage you've just read? What does this passage say about God's relationship with us? What does it say about His nature toward us? What have you learned about the Good Shepherd through what you've read?

Reading the Bible can sometimes feel like a lot of effort, but it all comes down to how you approach it. If you take an average of 10 to 15 minutes to read a passage each day, you can apply this method to your Bible study. All five steps shouldn't take longer than 20 minutes. That's a small portion of your day dedicated to Jesus. As time goes on, you can make it longer.

The more you read the Bible to retain and comprehend information, the more you'll begin to notice things you hadn't before. Reading the Bible won't earn you extra credit with God, but it will help you identify His voice. It will help you get nearer to Him. As you grow in knowledge of who God is, you become enveloped in His presence, allowing you to trust and know Him—in all seasons.

Reflect in Prayer

Prayer is a powerful resource. Once you've unpacked what God is communicating as you read the passage, it's time to reflect in prayer. Always start and end your devotional or Bible reading time with prayer. Jesus, as the Good Shepherd, outlines how we should pray using the *Lord's Prayer* as a guide in **Matthew 6:9–13**. You'll be amazed at what God reveals when you follow His guide for prayer.

Also, always keep your approach to devotionals manageable. Setting impossible goals for yourself will result in skipping your devotions altogether. For example, don't plan for 45 minutes to an hour of devotional time if you struggle to sit still for just 5 minutes. Instead, plan for 10 minutes so you can genuinely build from there. Choosing a topic or book of focus is also helpful to stay on track.

Having a regular time and place for devotion helps develop commitment. Find your pattern and constantly turn your heart toward God. A routine eventually becomes a comforting rhythm. It creates a sense of familiarity with God's voice and presence, making you return to seek more of Him.

And just because you have a routine established doesn't mean you should follow a monotonous pattern of doing things. The Good Shepherd is far from boring, so your routine can be fun. Don't be afraid to try something new occasionally. Be creative with the time you spend with Jesus so it can continue to excite you.

For example, you can spend your devotional time outside rather than constantly being cooped up at home. You can also write your prayers on colorful cards and place them in a jar to check at the end of each month. Keep things fun by taking prayer walks around your yard and intentionally looking for God's hand in nature. Also, introduce some good Christian music that speaks to how great God is.

When you return to God, the aim is to establish closeness with Him. The more fun you make your time with Jesus, the more likely you'll accomplish your aim. You just have to keep showing up, even when you don't feel good enough, eager, or worthy. You can trust God to show up faithfully as you keep bringing yourself to Him.

How to Get Up When You Fall

When you fall, get back up. Our faith walk will be filled with challenges and victories. There will be times when we follow Jesus, and times when we fall. But how we handle these challenges—maneuvering draining thoughts, strong emotions, and bad days—is what matters. Will you fall and rise again?

Pray With Purpose

Those of us who want to stand after falling need to put in the work. We can start by praying with purpose. In Eden, Adam and Eve show how people have the natural urge to hide from God when they fall. We are typically overwhelmed by shame and guilt, even though we shouldn't be. God is with us when we fall, and we should run to Him rather than hide from Him.

Something special happens when we pray with purpose and are honest with God after a fall. He offers us relief, peace, and help through the Holy Spirit. Going to God in prayer is an opportunity for humility and surrender. God is our great help. Falling doesn't scare the Good Shepherd away. If anything, it proves to us how much we can't do this life without Him.

We can fall into the trap of praying general prayers with no substance. However, we need to be specific with our prayers because the Good Shepherd is specific. The Bible says that when we pray, we should keep it simple and sincere, rather than babbling like pagans, saying many words (**The Holy Bible, New International Version, 2011/1973, Matthew 6:7**). Our general prayers can become babbling to God. We need to be purposeful and honest with what we bring to Him.

Also, Jesus knows our hearts already, so there's really nothing we can say that He isn't already aware of. God loves the details, and that's why He points out that we should be specific when we pray. He made creation and everything in the universe with intention. In fact, God even gave us 10 specific commandments in Exodus 20:1–21 to obey and live by. We were made in our mothers' womb with great intention and detail. In the same way, we should enter His presence with intention. When we do, He provides for what we need and offers permanent fixes.

Purposeful Prayer: ACTS Model

Purposeful prayer is the first step in faith. We trust that God is listening and that He cares enough to respond. God's Word says it best: "Before they call I will answer; while they are still speaking I will hear" (***The Holy Bible, New International Version, 2011/1973, Isaiah 65:24***). He is listening.

You can pray purposeful prayers using the ACTS model. ACTs is a prayer acronym that stands for adoration, confession, thanksgiving, and supplication. This approach to prayer can help you activate your faith. Don't drag your feet when you present yourself to Jesus; be quick to act.

Here's an example of how to use the ACTS model:

- **Adoration.** Always start prayer with adoration for God. Allow yourself to remember His goodness and be filled with wonder about His character. Remember that God always desires to be with you. Use Psalms 67 and 100 as guides for thanksgiving and praise. An example of adoration from the Lord's Prayer is: "Our Father who art in heaven, hallowed be thy name..."

- **Confession.** Then, repent. Ask God to reveal your sin and make you clean as you enter a holy conversation with Him. You can use 1 Peter 3:7 and Psalm 32:3–5 as guides for confession. An example of confession from the Lord's Prayer is: "Give us today our daily bread and forgive us our trespasses..."

- **Thanksgiving.** Next, give thanks at the feet of God. Thank Him for your blessings and the trials that you're overcoming. Make sure that you take nothing for granted. Use Thessalonians 5:18 as a guide for giving thanks to God. An example of thanksgiving is: "Thank you that you say in your word [mentioned a promise], and I believe that it is done..."

- **Supplication.** Finally, lift your worries to God. Pray about your desires and also bring the concerns of the people you love to Him. Pray for the needs of the nation and your family. Ask God to reveal who you should bring forward in prayer. Philippians 4:6–7 is a great passage to draw from for supplication.

Prayer helps you recount how worthy the Good Shepherd is of praise. It's truly a moment to lift His name higher than all others. You can pray as the Spirit guides, but remember to highlight God's attributes and nature.

Say who He is to you. More than asking God for stuff, prayer is about connecting with Him.

Praise God

Praise and worship God through song and by the way you live each day. Honoring God allows Him more access to you. Praise is a powerful resource that has a calming effect on us, reassuring and soothing us in times of anxiety. It can also confuse the enemy, especially when we do it during times of fall.

We are called to praise God at all times; His name should continually be on our lips (***The Holy Bible, New International Version, 2011/1973, Psalm 34:1***). There are plenty of reasons we should praise God. He is good, compassionate, loving, faithful, patient, full of grace, and merciful—to name a few. We need to praise Him for all things.

When we praise God, we turn our heads away from troubles and fix our gaze on Jesus. Praise isn't just for when things are going well; it should also be offered when things aren't so good. If anything, praising God is a form of surrender. It helps us move forward in faith and denounce fear. Praise is essential for reaffirming faith and building trust in Jesus.

You Are Found in Christ

Jesus wants us all to come to Him, and He embraces us. God's Word is full of promises, all of which are addressed to us. Each book in the Bible speaks to God's faithfulness, and in His goodness, Jesus seeks to extend this faithfulness to us. Whether we are in the pen, happily following the Good Shepherd, or in seasons of straying and falling, we can call on God's promises.

Like King David, we can ask the Lord to sustain us according to His promises and can plead with Him not to let our hopes be shattered (*The Holy Bible, New International Version,* **2011/1973, Psalm 119:116**). We can find solace in God and His Word in all situations because we are found in Christ.

Reflect on God's Promises

Many of us have been let down by someone we love. Disappointments are a part of life, especially when dealing with people. But the good news is Jesus is consistent. God is a promise keeper. He doesn't let us down or disappoint us because He keeps His word.

You can find God's promises throughout the Bible, so I encourage you to delve into His Word. Some Scriptures to help you start reflecting on God's promises include:

- Isaiah 40:31
- Jeremiah 29:11
- Proverbs 3:5–6
- John 14:1–3

Take a moment to turn to your Bible and reflect on these promises. This can be the start of your devotional time with God. Dive into these passages and let the Holy Spirit guide you.

His promises are intentional and directed at you. For example, God promises you His goodness, presence, provision, wisdom, sustenance, and so much more.

Rely on God

Before discussing marriage, couples invest time in learning about each other. You want to know who the person you are considering marriage with is, so you spend as much time with them as you can, carefully paying attention to their character. As the learning continues, the couple grows closer to each other and eventually arrives at true intimacy. Your relationship with Jesus is no different.

Relying on God is a period of learning and truly understanding the Good Shepherd's character, which helps us build lasting intimacy with Him. As we learn more about Jesus, we mature in our faith and become more likely to take Him at His word. When you take the time to truly get to know the Good Shepherd, you learn how much you can rely on Him. You see your prayers answered, and His presence becomes all the more apparent in your life. The more you rely on God, the more He moves in response to your faith.

Think of the woman with the issue of blood who had lived that way for 12 years (***The Holy Bible, New International Version, 2011/1973, Mark 5:25–34***). She pushed past crowds in faith, believing that if she could touch Jesus' garment, she would be healed. In this story, we see that the woman was right. When she touched Jesus, He felt power leave Him and asked, "Who touched me?" (***The Holy Bible, New International Version, 2011/1973, Mark 5:31***). The woman revealed herself, trembling before Jesus. At that point, Jesus told her: "Daughter, your faith has healed you. Go in peace and be freed from suffering" (***The Holy Bible, New International Version, 2011/1973, Mark 5:34***).

This woman's story is an example of complete reliance on God. The woman had lived with the issue of blood for so many years, and she probably tried all she could to heal it with her own remedies, knowledge, and might, none of which worked until Jesus. We should demonstrate the same desperation, if not more, that leads us to sort through crowds and undermine trends just so we can arrive at the Good Shepherd's garment. It's in our favor to reach for Him as the woman did and rely on His ability to do exceedingly above all that we could think or ask of Him (**refer to Ephesians 3:20**).

To rely on God is to be unafraid of what people will think or say about our decision to follow Him. It's to completely immerse ourselves in His promises, even when the situation says otherwise. For instance, the woman with the issue of blood had every reason to believe she would never be healed since she had lived with this condition for so many years. But she chose to trust in Jesus' promise. She had heard that "this man" (Jesus) could heal, so she took Him at His word. Had she not relied on God's promise, she would have robbed herself of the opportunity to exercise faith and receive her healing. Let us be willing to demonstrate our faith today and rely on God entirely.

Rely on God by Knowing His Promises

We need to know what God says He will do for us in order to trust Him for it. The woman with the issue of blood heard that Jesus was healing people, and she trusted that He could do the same for her if only she could be close enough to touch Him—and her faith was rewarded. We can only rely on God when we truly know His promises.

The Bible is God's Word for us, so we don't have to assume or be confused by what He has promised. It's all alive—open it up and dive into what He has said and continues to say. We do ourselves a great disservice if God's Word isn't the foundation of our lives. Let's immerse ourselves in Him through the Bible. Underline, repeat, memorize, contextualize, and meditate on the Scriptures daily. After all, you can't rely on God's promises unless you know them.

Rely on God by Testing His Promises

Again, the woman with the issue of blood tested God's promise of healing by making her way to where Jesus was, pushing through a crowd, and reaching out her hand in faith, touching His garment. We must do the same. To rely on God's promises, we must step out in faith, believing that He is faithful to do what He says He will do—at all times and in all situations. What do you need to reach out to God in faith for today? What biblical promise covers what you desire? For many, finances are a tremendous need. Maybe you are reading this with very little money in your account. You could be worrying about next month's rent or other upcoming bills. But God is with you there, too.

He promises to provide in Scriptures such as Genesis 22:14, Philippians 4:19, Matthew 6:31–32, Psalm 145:15–16, and so many more. You must decide if you believe God is your provider, regardless of what your bank account looks like.

Then, test His promise by faithfully continuing to do what God has called you to—keep showing up to work, tithe your best to Him, give what you can to the poor, honor the Lord with what you can, budget wisely, buy only what you need, and so on. As with the woman of blood, your belief in God's promises must be backed up by your faith. It's helpful to act and move in ways that test the promise and create an environment for your faith to be rewarded.

We have to put our head knowledge of God into action by faith so that our understanding of His promises becomes a lived experience. Jesus doesn't just want us to *know* what He can do. Instead, He wants us to be living proof of His power at work in us through the Holy Spirit. Don't miss an opportunity to step out in faith and trust God to work things out for good.

Rely on God by Praying His Promises

God spoke the universe into existence, which means there's power in confession. In Christ, we have the authority to bring Heaven to earth by using our words. The Bible is clear that we bear the consequences of our words, for what we say can create (***The Holy Bible, New International Version, 2011/1973, Proverbs 18:21***). We can speak to create life or usher in death, so speak life over your situation. You might think, *But I don't know what to say*. Well, that's what God's promises are for. Replace your words with biblical declarations centered around what God says. When you pray, ensure that His promises are at the forefront of what you are trusting Him for.

Every prayer should acknowledge who God is, His sovereignty, and what He can do (**Schmidt, n.d.**). Then, pray for His will to be done in your life.

For example, "Dear Father in Heaven, you are worthy of all praise and honor. Your name is above every name, and you are all-powerful to transform all situations according to your will. Lord, the financial burden has been heavy on me this year. I feel overstretched with everything happening at home and being the sole provider for my family. But I know you haven't brought me this far to leave me and you who began a good work in me are faithful to complete it (*The Holy Bible, New International Version,* **2011/1973, Philippians 1:6**). I know your plans for me are for hope, prosperity, and to give me a bright future (*The Holy Bible, New International Version,* **2011/1973, Jeremiah 29:11**). I know you are the ultimate provider, and you will satisfy me beyond what my bank account can do. You promise to supply every need, including this one, according to your glory in Jesus Christ (*The Holy Bible, New International Version,* **2011/1973, Philippians 4**:19). And God, I believe you. I trust your promises to fulfill good plans in my life, provide for me, and never forsake me. Thank you for the strength you have instilled in me to keep going and act in faith. Thank you for your provision. I will continue to trust you. In the mighty name of Jesus Christ, I pray. Amen."

The example above demonstrates how you can incorporate God's promises in your conversations with Him. Always pray, and don't be discouraged. The Good Shepherd is always with you, even in hard seasons. The Bible says we will have challenges in this life, but we must be courageous and faithful because Jesus overcame the world (*The Holy Bible, New International Version,* **2011/1973, John 16:33**). Praying His promises is an impactful way of reminding ourselves that we will overcome because of who God is and what He says to us.

Rely on God by Trusting His Promises

Submit your plans to God and hold on to His promises. Trust in Him with all your heart in everything you do and have faith that "He will make your paths straight" because He will (*The Holy Bible, New International Version,* **2011/1973, Proverbs 3:5–6**). Relying on God means recklessly abandoning your own thoughts about the situation. No matter how scary or challenging something may feel or look to you, all is possible when God is in it. Trusting God's promises is a willful submission of your will under His. Let Him move into your life without trying to limit Him to what you know. Stop viewing what He can do through a restricted lens. Trusting God is saying, "I want you and believe you with all my heart." After all, it's only in Christ that we move, live, and have our being, so why wouldn't we rely on Him? (*The Holy Bible, New International Version,* **2011/1973, Acts 17:28**).

Let's make this a bit more personal. Imagine being in a relationship, and your partner says, "I love you with parts of my heart." I'm sure you'd feel very insecure about trusting them to love you for the long haul. But if your partner is clear that they love you wholeheartedly, it's easier to trust them with the future. Of course, God is bigger than any earthly relationship we could ever have, but this example highlights the power of being all in. Jesus is all in with us.

We have the opportunity to love God "because He first loved us" (*The Holy Bible, New International Version,* **2011/1973, 1 John 4:19**). The Good Shepherd is sure about us. As a partner who is clear about their intentions, God says, "Before I formed you in the womb I knew you, before you were born I set you apart; I appointed you as a prophet to the nations" (*The Holy Bible, New International Version,* **2011/1973, Jeremiah 1:5**). He created us knowing we would stray, fall, run, and everything in between, yet He chose to love us still. And while we were living deeply in sin, Jesus sacrificed Himself for us, as He does daily. There's no greater love than this!

The reality of who God is and who He chooses to be for us is reason enough to rely on Him and trust His promises. Trusting Him is a steady process of continual surrender. We must obey His Word and live according to His commandments. It benefits us to rest assured that God's promises will always take us where we need to go.

Rely on God by Resting in His Promises

Relying on God and knowing His promises brings rest. We can rest in what He says, knowing that He is faithful in doing it. Worry, however, is the opposite of rest. So when we find ourselves tossing and turning, concerned about what's coming next, it may be that our trust is not in God's promises.

When we turn our eyes to God's promises, we demonstrate complete reliance on Him. This pulls us out of the worrying state and places us in the hands of peace—not just any peace, but God's peace, which surpasses all understanding (***The Holy Spirit, New International Version,* 2011/1973, Philippians 4:**7). As Jesus' sheep, we are blessed with a Good Shepherd who tells us not to worry and give our concerns over to Him.

Resting in God's promises adds more to our lives than worry ever could. We need to get into the habit of turning our concerns over to Him. The Bible encourages us not to worry about life, what to drink, what to eat, or even what we will wear because God takes care of us (***The Holy Bible, New International Version,* 2011/1973, Matthew 6:25**). Nature around us is an example of God's provision. He dresses the flowers in the field, feeds the birds in the sky, and promises to do much more than that for us.

We should begin to apply God's promises to our lives. The daily strategy for relying on God is to retain His promises in our minds. Whatever we meditate on, we eventually believe, and it seeps into our hearts, translating into our actions and choices.

God's got this. Whether you have a financial need, are dealing with fear, or need help with decision-making, leave it in His hands. We can trust Him, rest in Him, and rely on His Word. God's promises are meant to lead us to live a full, satisfying life in Him—one that is enjoyable and best represents Him.

Conclusion

The world is constantly seeking to devour Jesus' sheep through trends, worldly cultures, and damaging habits, which is why we need Jesus to take the load off us. As Jesus' sheep, we are called to move and follow Him, but we are bound to stray, stumble, and fall. Even so, God wants us all the more. He wants to change our ways to reflect His own so that we can live abundant lives in Him.

Christ cares for the sheep who are near and intimate with Him as much as He does for those finding their way to Him. Unlike people who often disappoint and don't keep their word, God never fails us. He chooses us every day and invites us all into His presence. The Good Shepherd provides for His sheep. He nourishes, helps, instructs, and frees us. No matter where we are in our walk with God, He cares for us because of who He is.

Knowing that the Good Shepherd always leads to good news. It means we don't have to walk the road of lost sheep. We can immerse ourselves in His direction, instruction, and love. Walking with Jesus means we no longer have to feel alone or clueless. The Good Shepherd provides the map for where we should go and how we can live fruitful lives.

The best thing anyone can do for themselves is to draw near to the Good Shepherd, for following Jesus is the best decision we can make.

God's Word is unchanging, and the One who speaks it is reliable. His Word isn't dependent on our feelings or the situation in front of us. Instead, what God says remains the ultimate truth, regardless of the circumstances or how we feel about them. Of course, in His goodness, Jesus isn't shocked when we stray, sleep, or fall. He always makes provisions for us. Even in our toughest times, the distance we create for ourselves doesn't stop Him from wanting us. Jesus longs for us to return home, no matter how many times we pull away from Him.

The enemy wants to tire us out, but the Good Shepherd calls us to wisdom. We need to wake up from spiritual sleep and recognize our authority in Christ to win over the things of this world. God is not surprised by our mistakes.

Whether we run from God out of fear, laziness, or pride, we are still purposed for something great. Much like Jonah, God will send what He needs to, including discomfort, to bring us back to our place in Him. Jesus is always ready and willing to embrace us when we repent and return to His loving arms.

It's also okay if we fall, but we must choose to get back up every time—not from self-condemnation, but from a place of knowing Jesus' love. Remember, the fall is preparation. Depending on how we respond to the season, it can strengthen our faith.

You may not be perfect, but God is not seeking perfection. He is looking for you to walk alongside the Good Shepherd daily. Do not miss the opportunity to live in grace and have faith in God. The reward of worldly pursuits is temporary, but God's reward lasts for eternity.

The road to the Father is narrow because the world doesn't know they can be found in Him. Jesus has already laid down His life for us all and invites us to choose Him as He has chosen us. So, we should approach everything with eternity in mind.

Believer or nonbeliever, we are all on a timeline, and those who submit their lives to Christ get to enjoy the reward with Him in Heaven. Let's not miss out on the life-changing chance to be with the Good Shepherd by satisfying temporary desires. It is within our power to decide to accept Jesus as our Good Shepherd, the Lord and Savior of our lives. We are blessed to be able to lean on God for everything. After all, Jesus Christ is the way, the truth, and the life; all we'll ever need is found in Him.

This book offers plenty of ways to start your journey of following Jesus. It also offers resources to use when you stray, sleep, run, or fall. Remember, you are always found in Christ, so delve into God's Word, pray, and actively build intimacy with Him—don't let up.

Use the ACTS approach to start and end each day in prayer. Choose your company wisely, create spiritual boundaries, submit yourself, repent every time you fall, and get close to the Shepherd. You can also use the SOAP Bible study method to make the most of your quality time with the Good Shepherd. If you make time for Jesus and are persistent in knowing Him, He will always be real and tangible in your life. The Good Shepherd is willing and waiting for you. Will you seek Him today? I challenge you to accept His invitation to find your purpose right now.

About the Author

Jeff Gwaltney is the founder and lead pastor of One Seed Church in St. Louis, Missouri. He holds a bachelor's degree in business administration from Belmont University and a master's degree in theology from Vanguard University. He graduated from Jakes Divinity School, founded by current chancellor Bishop TD Jakes. He is an established recording artist, songwriter, producer, author, and ordained minister of the Gospel. Pastor Jeff and his family live in the St. Louis area.

References

A Little Butterfly. (2023, July 18). *Nothing can stop God's plan for your life.* Medium. https://medium.com/@writerbutterfly/nothing-can-stop-gods-plan-for-your-life-270bfb5328bc

Akrotirianakis, S. (2020, September 15). *Psalm 100—we are the sheep of his pasture.* OCN. https://myocn.net/psalm-100-we-are-the-sheep-of-his-pasture/

Amazing Grace. (n.d.). Hymnal.net. https://www.hymnal.net/en/hymn/h/313

Anderson, C. (2022, July 15). *Doing my God assignment today–It's as simple as that.* Missionary Life. https://missionarylife.org/god-assignment-missionary-life/

Anderson, J. N. (2017, June 27). *Why did God allow the fall?* TGC. https://www.thegospelcoalition.org/article/why-did-god-allow-the-fall/

Angley, E. (2008, April). *You don't win the battle by running away.* Ernest Agley Ministries. https://ernestangley.org/read/article/you_dont_win_the_battle_by_running_away

Antwi, D. (2021, April 15). *Spiritually asleep? 5 ways to wake up from spiritual slumber.* LinkedIn. https://www.linkedin.com/pulse/spiritually-asleep-5-ways-wake-up-from-spiritual-slumber-antwi

Are you running away from God? (n.d.). Our Daily Bread. https://ourdailybread.org/article/are-you-running-away-from-god/

Arimborgo, J. (2023, October 5). *Do you feel deeply safe?* Feeding on Jesus. https://feedingonjesus.com/2023/10/05/do-you-feel-deeply-safe/

Arlene. (2017, September 13). *Overcoming the spirit of slumber.* Walk Whole. https://walkwhole.com/2017/09/13/overcoming-the-spirit-of-slumber/

Arnel, R. (2023, August 25). *3 reasons why Jesus is worth following.* Christ Fellowship Church. https://www.christfellowship.church/articles/3-reasons-why-jesus-is-worth-following

Baurain, B. (2021, July 14). *The sheep of his pasture.* Today in the Word. https://www.todayintheword.org/daily-devotional/following-the-good-shepherd/the-sheep-of-his-pasture/

Begg, A. (2024, April 28). *Jesus lifts us up.* Truth for Life. https://www.truthforlife.org/devotionals/alistair-begg/4/28/2024/

Bethesda Senior Living. (2022, February 3). *5 ways to enrich your daily walk with the Lord.* The Gardens at Collinwood. https://www.collinwoodco.com/blog/5-ways-to-enrich-your-daily-walk-with-the-lord

Borgman, B. (2019, September 6). *God cares about how you feel.* Core Christianity. https://corechristianity.com/resources/articles/god-cares-about-how-you-feel

Burt, T. (2020, Januray 29). *God's power working in you!* Tim Burt. https://timburt.org/2020/01/29/gods-power-working-in-you/

Cain, T. (2016, October 8). *God will accomplish his purpose (Isaiah 46:9–10[11]).* Fighter Verses.

https://www.fighterverses.com/post/god-will-accomplish-his-purpose-is-46-9-11

Chadwick, D., & Chadwick, M. (2021, June 9). *Davidisms – rejection is God's redirection.* Moments of Hope Church. https://www.momentsofhopechurch.org/post/davidisms-rejection-is-god-s-redirection

Chase, M. L. (2023, June 17). *10 things you should know about the fall.* Crossway. https://www.crossway.org/articles/10-things-you-should-know-about-the-fall/

Chelette, R. (n.d.). *Failure isn't fatal with Jesus.* Living Hope. https://www.livehope.org/devotional/failure-isnt-fatal-with-jesus/

Chery. (n.d.). *How to get back to Jesus after a fall.* The Christian Alarm. https://www.thechristianalarm.com/how-to-get-back-to-jesus/

Clarke, A. (n.d.). *What does an encounter with God really look like?* Catch the Fire. https://www.catchthefire.com/blog/encountering-god-look-like

Cooper, H. (2021, August 27). *5 powerful steps to align with God's purpose.* My One Comfort. https://myonecomfort.com/5-powerful-steps-to-align-with-gods-purpose/amp/

Copeland, K. (n.d.). *From faith to faith—daily devotional.* Kenneth Copeland Ministries. https://www.kcm.org/read/faith-to-faith/07/30?language_content_entity=en-US

Copp, S. (2022, March 29). *Choosing God over this world.* Having God. https://havinggod.com/choosing-god-over-this-world/

Coxall, P. (2020, July 8). *The importance of self-control.* UTG. https://understandingthegospel.org/blogs/paul-coxall/the-importance-of-self-control/

Davidson, E. (2019, January 3). *The purpose of the wilderness in the lives of God's people.* Findsoulrest. https://findsoulrest.com/2019/01/03/the-purpose-of-the-wilderness-in-the-lives-of-gods-people/

DeMarco, D. (2024, August 29). *What Christ taught us in the Garden of Gethsemane.* National Catholic Register. https://www.ncregister.com/commentaries/christ-taught-us-garden-of-gethsemane

Demers, S. (2021, August 16). *10–"Pride goes before a fall..." the value of humility.* Lighthouse. https://www.lighthouse-ministries.org/sermons/10-pride-goes-before-a-fall-the-value-of-humility/

d'Entremont, L. (2018, July 19). *How to walk by faith and not by your feelings.* Crosswalk.com. https://www.crosswalk.com/faith/spiritual-life/faith-over-feelings.html

Discovering true life in Jesus. (n.d.). Chosen Gen Ministry. https://chosengenministry.org/true-life-found-in-jesus

Does your fear lead to disobedience? (2021, February 19). Balanced Living Body & Spirit. https://www.getsomebalance.com/news/2021/2/19/does-your-fear-lead-to-disobedience

Domangue, P. (n.d.). *Remember God and His work in your life because it matters for your today.* On Fire Ministries. https://www.onfire-ministries.org/blog/remember-god

Drendel, K. (2020, April 13).*God meets us where we are.* Navigating by Faith. https://navigatingbyfaith.com/2020/04/13/god-meets-us-where-we-are/

Ellis, P. (2013, April 10). *What happens when we stray?* Escape to Reality. https://escapetoreality.org/2013/04/10/what-happens-to-christians-who-stray/

Eternal life there's more to it than you think. (n.d.). Andrew Woman Ministries. https://www.awmi.net/reading/teaching-articles/eternal_life/

Evans, K. (2023, February 13). *Does Jesus love me?* Ligonier. https://www.ligonier.org/learn/articles/does-jesus-love-me?srsltid=AfmBOoqOp8AJz-2GPWLH3UYfo9lnYxh9dr11qXoyWpI5beTVc06zzrA_

Faith in Jesus Christ. (n.d.). Church of Jesus Christ. https://www.churchofjesuschrist.org/study/manual/gospel-topics/faith-in-jesus-christ?lang=eng

Farris, S. (2020, July 28). *Being resilient falling and rising back up.* Crossroads. https://crossroadcoach.com/being-resilient/

Ference, D. (2020, December 1). *What Peter and Christ teach us about dealing with past sins.* Word on Fire. https://www.wordonfire.org/articles/fellows/what-peter-and-christ-teach-us-about-dealing-with-past-sins/

First15. (2019, November 19). *The parable of the Good Shepherd.* Praise.com. https://www.praise.com/devotional/the-parable-of-the-good-shepherd

The flesh is weak (Matthew 26:36–46). (n.d.). Saraland Christians. https://saralandchristians.com/sermons/2021/12/7/the-flesh-is-weak-matthew-2636-46

Franklin, J. (2019, July 14). *Your failure is not final.* Jentezen Franklin. https://jentezenfranklin.org/connection-questions/your-failure-is-not-final-2

Fredrickson, J. (n.d.). *How to pray woth the ACTS prayer model (Adoration, contrition, thankfulness, supplication)*. Hallow. https://hallow.com/blog/how-to-pray-acts/

Furman, D. (2018, Feberuary 28). *If God loves you, He will prune you*. TGC. https://www.thegospelcoalition.org/article/god-prunes-those-he-loves/

Gardner, N. (2022, March 8). *Three encouragements for pastors pursuing wandering sheep*. 9Marks. https://www.9marks.org/article/three-encouragements-for-pastors-pursuing-wandering-sheep/

Gaultiere, B. (n.d.). *Jesus' solitude and silence*. Soul Shepherding. https://www.soulshepherding.org/jesus-solitude-and-silence/

Generation Church. (2021, January 11). *Running from your calling | Jonah | Ryan Visconti* [Video]. YouTube. https://www.youtube.com/watch?v=LidlNec1UmE

Giffard, P. (n.d.). *Article—What does it mean to have a personal relationship with Jesus?* Diocese of Pembroke. https://pembrokediocese.com/article/what-does-it-mean-to-have-a-personal-relationship-with-jesus/

Giovanelli, T. (2021, January 12). *Spirit of self-control sermon 2 Timothy 1:7*. Life Church. https://manlylife.org/2021/01/12/spirit-of-self-control-sermon-2-timothy-17/

Gladwell, M. (n.d.). *The shepherd motif in the Old and New Testament*. Dwell Community Church. https://www.dwellcc.org/essays/shepherd-motif-old-and-new-testament

God's promises are for all His kids, even you. (n.d.). Newspring Church. https://newspring.cc/devotionals/trusting-gods-promises-a-7-day-devotional/gods-promises-are-for-all-his-kids-even-you

God's promises never fail. (n.d.). Newspring Church. https://newspring.cc/devotionals/trusting-gods-promises-a-7-day-devotional/gods-promises-never-fail

Going Beyond Ministries with Priscilla Shirer. (2024, January 3). *Priscilla Shirer | Remember God's promises and hold on to His peace* [Video]. YouTube. https://www.youtube.com/watch?v=RiQd4gRol1Y

Goodling, K. (2018, July 6). *Five things you should know about sheep behavior.* Living With Gotlands. https://www.livingwithgotlands.com/2018/07/five-things-you-should-know-about-sheep-behavior/?cn-reloaded=1

Graham, B. (n.d.). *Sin.* Going Farther. https://goingfarther.net/basics-of-christianity/sin/

Griffin, A. (2023, December 29). *3 practical ways to walk by faith and not by sight.* Christianity.com. https://www.christianity.com/wiki/christian-life/practical-ways-to-walk-by-faith-and-not-by-sight.html

Gross, J. (2024, June 10). *Fruit of the Spirit: Self-control through the love of Christ.* Blog. https://blog.cph.org/read/fruit-of-the-spirit-self-control

Hamilton, I. (2024, June 21). *How is Jesus the good shepherd?* Ligonier. https://www.ligonier.org/learn/articles/how-is-jesus-the-good-shepherd?srsltid=AfmBOoqPIGjl84-jlTTyVxbYn_rOeaHdsQ-uqi2TLvECCk4JnbPoYusx

Harrison, D. (2016, July 26). *Lessons from a sheep, part 5, I've fallen, and I can't get up.* Moving On: Surviving the Grief of Forced Termination. http://deannaharrison.com/2016/07/26/lessons-from-a-sheep-part-5-ive-fallen-and-i-cant-get-up/

Hetrick, L. (2013, May 14). *God's will and your big, stupid mistakes—4 things to remember.* Average Us. https://averageus.com/2013/05/14/gods-will-and-your-big-stupid-mistakes-4-things-to-remember/

Hobbs, D. (2015, October 20). *Your daily cup of inspiration.* Diana Hobbs. https://www.diannahobbs.com/dianna_hobbs_empowering_e/2015/10/there-is-no-failure-in-god.html

The Holy Bible, New International Version. (2011). YouVersion. https://www.bible.com/versions/111-niv-new-international-version (Original work published 1973).

Hopler, W. (2020, November 19). *5 ways to wake up when you're spiritually asleep.* Crosswalk.com. https://www.crosswalk.com/faith/spiritual-life/ways-to-wake-up-when-youre-spiritually-asleep.html

Hopler, W. (2024, September 16). *7 Bible verses about God's provision during autumn.* Crosswalk.com. https://www.crosswalk.com/slideshows/bible-verses-about-gods-provision-during-autumn.html

Horst, J. M. (2023, May 4). *God preserves his people.* Heralds of Hope. https://heraldsofhope.org/blog/all-episodes/god-preserves-his-people/

Hottle, J. (2022, December 28). *Feeling safe with God.* Jessica Hottle. https://www.jessicahottle.com/safe-with-god/

How do we return to intimacy with God after we stray? (2015, January 19). Verse by Verse Ministry. https://versebyverseministry.org/bible-answers/how-do-we-return-to-intimacy-with-god-after-we-stray?locale=en

How to remember what you read in the Bible. (n.d.). Delighting in Jesus. https://onethingalone.com/remember-what-you-read-in-the-bible/

Is there forgiveness for repeated failure? (n.d.). Every Woman a Theologian. https://phyliciamasonheimer.com/failure-forgiveness-sin/

I surrender my failure. (n.d.). Prison Fellowship. https://www.prisonfellowship.org/resources/training-resources/mentoring-ministry/surrender-bible-verses-on-failure/

Jackson, S. D. (2023, November 29). *Jesus is the good shepherd—why this is important.* Shirley Desmond Jackson. https://shirleydesmondjackson.com/jesus-is-the-good-shepherd-why-this-is-important/

Jarrett, E. (2024, November 10). *To be found in Christ.* Medium. https://medium.com/a-clay-jar/to-be-found-in-christ-06fba79e797b

Jesus is the good shepherd who leads and protects his sheep. (2013, February 24). Revival Ministries International. https://www.revival.com/a/4694-jesus-is-the-good-shepherd-who-leads-and-protects-his-sheep

Jesus' response when you fall. (2024, March 14). Seminole Community Church. https://www.seminolechurch.com/jesus-response-when-you-fall

John. (n.d.). The good shepherd's love—John 10:11–21. *Providence Presbyterian Church.* https://www.provroanoke.org/blog/good-shepherds-love

Jones, C. (2019, April 15). *Live with your eyes open.* Desiring God. https://www.desiringgod.org/articles/live-with-your-eyes-open

Jones, E. (n.d.). *God will preserve you.* Life, Hope, & Truth. https://lifehopeandtruth.com/bible/blog/god-will-preserve-you/

Kaiser, D. (2021, April 21). *Even if I fail, God is faithful.* Revive Ministries. https://experiencerevival.com/2021/04/21/even-if-i-fail-god-is-faithful/

Kercheville, B. (n.d.). *Abundance in Christ.* West Palm Beach. https://westpalmbeachchurchofchrist.com/topical/christian_living/abundance_in_christ.html

Kight, T. (2018, December 10). *The discipline of discernment.* A Call to Excellence. https://www.acalltoexcellence.com/the-discipline-of-discernment/

Klinge, D. (2016, October 5). *5 qualities that make Jesus the good shepherd.* Dawn Klinge. https://www.dawnklinge.com/abovethewaves/5-qualities-that-make-jesus-the-good-shepherd

Larson, S. (n.d.). *God is preparing you for great things.* Faith Radio. https://www.myfaithradio.com/2015/god-is-preparing-you-for-great-things/

Leake, M. (2022, March 24). *What is salvation? (Also: Why it's needed and how to get it).* Crosswalk.com. https://www.crosswalk.com/faith/spiritual-life/what-is-salvation-also-why-it-s-needed-and-how-to-get-it.html

LifeCoach4God. (2012, November 5). *God's 3 powers at work within us from Ephesians 3:20–21 by Crawford W. Loritts JR.* Lifecoach4God. https://lifecoach4god.life/2012/11/05/gods-3-powers-at-work-within-us-from-ephesians-320-21-by-crawford-w-loritts-jr/

Ling, M. (n.d.). *Your guide to coming back to God after falling away | Parable of the lost son.* Truthfully Michelle. https://truthfullymichelle.com/coming-back-to-god-after-falling-away/

Long, B. (2023, July 23). *I chose Jesus (but he chose me first).* Theology and Life. https://theology-and-life.com/2023/07/23/i-chose-jesus-but-he-chose-me-first/comment-page-1/

Loudermilk, M. (2023, December 13). *The shepherd and his sheep.* More to Life Today. https://www.moretolifetoday.net/the-shepherd-and-his-sheep/

Lou Redding, M. (n.d.). *How to have a daily devotional time.* The Upper Room. https://www.upperroom.org/resources/how-to-have-a-daily-devotional-time

Marva. (n.d.). *An intimate portrait of the God who pursues you.* Sun Sparkle Shine. https://sunsparkleshine.com/god-pursues-you/

Mathis, D. (2014, October 8). *Self-control and the power of Christ.* Desiring God. https://www.desiringgod.org/articles/self-control-and-the-power-of-christ

Mathis, D. (2021, November 16). *Do you insult your Savior's bride?* Desiring God. https://www.desiringgod.org/articles/do-you-insult-your-saviors-bride

McCauley, P. (2019, April 30). *The need for salvation.* Understanding the Gospel. https://understandingthegospel.org/explore-the-gospel/salvation/the-need-for-salvation/

McElroy, J. S. (n.d.). *Resisting your calling can lead to depression.* J Scott Mcelory. https://jscottmcelroy.com/resisting-your-calling-leads-to-depression/

McGarry, M. (March 2024). *Are all sins equal?* Youth Pastor Theologian. https://www.youthpastortheologian.com/blog/are-all-sins-equal

McMenamin, C. (2021, June 17). *What is the ACTS prayer method and how do you pray it?* Crosswlak.com. https://www.crosswalk.com/faith/prayer/what-is-the-acts-prayer-method-and-how-do-you-pray-it.html

Meeting Jesus in a quiet place. (n.d.). Candyce Carden. https://candycecarden.com/meeting-jesus-in-a-quiet-place/

Meyer, J. (n.d.). *The fruit of God's pruning process.* Joyce Meyer Ministries. https://joycemeyer.org/Grow-Your-Faith/Articles/The-Fruit-of-Gods-Pruning-Process

Mitchum, J. (2021, February 1). *Why do we need salvation?* Biblword. https://www.biblword.net/why-do-we-need-salvation/

Moore, T. B. (2023, September 1). *Walking in your purpose.* The Euclid Observer. https://www.theeuclidobserver.com/articles/walking-in-your-purpose/

Morgan, B. (2016, February 14). *A shepherd knows his sheep (Luke 15:1–7; John 10:24–28).* Way of Grace Church. https://www.wayofgracechurch.com/sermons/sermon/2016-02-14/a-shepherd-knows-his-sheep-luke-15:1-7-john-10:24-28

Morris, M. (2015, January). *Why is Jesus Christ important in my life?* The Church of Jesus Christ of Latter-Day Saints. https://www.churchofjesuschrist.org/study/new-era/2015/01/why-is-jesus-christ-important-in-my-life?lang=eng

Motl, A. (2024, September 26). *What does it mean that God is Jehovah-Jireh?* Christianity.com.

https://www.christianity.com/wiki/god/what-does-it-mean-that-god-is-jehovah-jireh.html

Mr. Streetz. (2023, April 10). *God wants you to diligently seek (search for) Him.* The Langford Files. https://thelangfordfiles.com/2023/04/10/god-wants-you-to-diligently-seek-search-for-him/

The need for salvation. (2024, July 7). In Touch Ministries. https://www.intouch.org/read/daily-devotions/the-need-for-salvation

Nelson, M. C. (2020, March 22). *Reasons to stay in your church.* Come to Christ. https://cometochrist.ca/reasons-to-stay-in-your-church/

Newheiser, J. (2020, September 17). *3 lessons from David's fall and forgiveness.* TGC. https://www.thegospelcoalition.org/article/3-lessons-david-fall-forgiveness/

Ocermiller, T. (2021, May 14). *My shepherd guides me through the valley.* LinkedIn. https://www.linkedin.com/pulse/my-shepherd-guides-me-through-valley-thomas-overmiller

Omondi, B. (2023, September 25). *Simple way to align your intentions with God's will (Real life story included).* Medium. https://medium.com/@bernardomondi2020/simple-way-to-align-your-intentions-with-gods-will-real-life-story-included-4c60de097d99

Once we were lost: what it means to be found in Christ. (n.d.). Alyssa J Howard. https://www.alyssajhoward.com/2018/10/20/found-in-christ/

O'Neal, S. G. (2020, July 13). *4 reasons you may be feeling far from God.* Daily She Pursues. https://dailyshepursues.com/4-reasons-you-may-be-feeling-far-from-god/

One Seed with Jeff Gwaltney. (2024, May 29). *Jesus sheep - follow | Pastor Jeff Gwaltney | One Seed Church* [Video]. YouTube. https://www.youtube.com/watch?v=E_o91-Ntpko

One Seed with Jeff Gwaltney. (2024, June 4). *Jesus shee - stray | Pastor Jeff Gwaltney | One Seed Church* [Video]. YouTube. https://www.youtube.com/watch?v=Nl3kpTz9Orw

One Seed with Jeff Gwaltney. (2024, June 11). *Jesus sheep - sleep | Pastor Jeff Gwaltney | One Seed Church* [Video]. YouTube. https://www.youtube.com/watch?v=319J8L6HTpU

One Seed with Jeff Gwaltney. (2024, June 18). *Jesus sheep - run | Pastor Jeff Gwaltney | One Seed Church* [Video]. YouTube. https://www.youtube.com/watch?v=PuSm4cudeL4

One Seed with Jeff Gwaltney. (2024, June 26). *Jesus sheep - fall | Pastor Jeff Gwaltney | One Seed Church* [Video]. YouTube. https://www.youtube.com/watch?v=zDW_AdUVyN0

One Seed with Jeff Gwaltney. (2024, July 2). *Jesus sheep - found | Pastor Jeff Gwaltney | One Seed Church* [Video]. YouTube. https://www.youtube.com/watch?v=zEM6Ypvhugc

Our failures are not fatal. (n.d.). The Christian Working Woman. https://christianworkingwoman.org/broadcasts/our-failures-are-not-fatal/

Owensby, J. (2021, June 16). *Being patient with yourself.* Ministry Matters. https://www.ministrymatters.com/all/entry/10817/being-patient-with-yourself

Pardoe, S. (2018, September 26). *The secret no one tells you in your lowest moment.* Stacey Pardoe. https://staceypardoe.com/2018/09/26/lowest-moment-open-door-god-work/

Parkman, K. (2023, December 12). *An intentional God.* Disciple Daily. https://discipledaily.org/blog/2023/12/12/an-intentional-god

Parnell, J. (n.d.). *The watchful man.* Cities Church. https://www.citieschurch.com/journal/the-watchful-man

Parnell, J. (2013, January 21). *To be found in Christ (Philippians 3:9).* Fighter Verses. https://www.fighterverses.com/post/to-be-found-in-christ

Paul, I. (2023, October 20). *What is it like to encounter Jesus?* Psephizo. https://www.psephizo.com/biblical-studies/what-is-it-like-to-encounter-jesus/

Pauley, S. (2020, September 11). *Regathering the flock.* Enjoying the Journey. https://enjoyingthejourney.org/regathering-the-flock/

Paulgaard, J. (2024, May 30). *Walking with the Shepherd.* James Paulgaard. https://jamespaulgaard.com/2024/05/30/walking-with-the-shepherd/

Paul's letters to churches. (n.d.). River View Church. https://rivchurch.com/study-guide/thread/pauls-letters-to-churches/

Perritt, A. (n.d.). *When you believe the lies instead of the truth.* Love God Greatly. https://lovegodgreatly.com/lgg-posts/believe-lies-instead-truth/

Phillips, R. (2014, September 29). *God is faithful to preserve his own.* Ligonier. https://www.ligonier.org/learn/articles/god-faithful-preserve-his-own

Piper, J. (1988, November 20). *Battling the unbelief of bitterness.* Desiring God. https://www.desiringgod.org/messages/battling-the-unbelief-of-bitterness

Piper, J. (2008, May 26). *Why can't I overcome my bitterness and anger?* Desiring God. https://www.desiringgod.org/interviews/why-cant-i-overcome-my-bitterness-and-anger

Piper, J. (2016, April 29). *What is worship?* Desiring God. https://www.desiringgod.org/interviews/what-is-worship

Piper, J. (2020, May 8). *What is grace?* Desiring God. https://www.desiringgod.org/interviews/what-is-grace

The power of patience in waiting. (n.d.). In Due Time. https://www.in-due-time.com/faith/the-power-of-patience-in-waiting/

The power that works in you. (n.d.). Christ Embassy. https://christembassy.org/the-power-that-works-in-you/

Prewitt, P. (2022, July 10). *"Sometimes, God has to break you down to build you back up."* Un-associated. https://www.un-associated.com/sometimes-god-has-to-break-you-down-to-build-you-back-up/

Prewitt, P. (2023, August 20). *We live in a world where temptation is real, a society that tells us to conform to its way of living which is the opposite o God's, and a body.* Un-associated. https://www.un-associated.com/can-we-continue-living-in-sin/

Pullis, S. (2020, June 25). *What is a personal relationship with Jesus?* Unleash The Gospel. https://www.unleashthegospel.org/2020/06/what-is-a-personal-relationship-with-jesus/

Pursuing Jesus in solitude. (2019, May 9). Hour of Power. https://hourofpower.org/pursuing-jesus-in-solitude/

Ramsey Solutions. (2024, May 9). *How to get closer to God.* Ramsey Solutions. https://www.ramseysolutions.com/personal-growth/how-to-get-closer-to-god

Reddy, S. (2022, October 13). *Why do we run and hide from God?* The Good Christian. https://www.thegoodchristian.co/blog/why-do-we-run-and-hide-from-god

Reinemann, M. (2024, November 12). *Spiritual sleep.* The Mind of Christ. https://seekinghismind.com/articles/2022/1/14/spiritual-sleep

Returning to God through scripture. (n.d.). Oak Cliff Bible Fellowship. https://www.ocbfchurch.org/returning-to-god-through-scripture/

Rice, C. (2023, April 6). *Trusting God in the storm: Finding hope in hard times.* Carolynsbooks. https://carolynsbooks.com/trusting-god-in-the-storm-finding-hope-in-hard-times/

Rotzoll, T. (n.d.). *Aligning your goals with God's will.* Footprints of Inspiration. https://www.footprintsofinspiration.com/aligning-your-goals-with-gods-will/

Ryan, M. (2023, October 27). *Finding God's provision in unexpected places.* Proverbs 31. https://proverbs31.org/read/devotions/full-post/2023/10/27/finding-gods-provision-in-unexpected-places

Santiago, G. (2020, April 9). *All we need is in Christ.* Living Revelations. https://livingrevelations.com/all-we-need-is-in-christ/

Saul (Paul) becomes a Christian. (n.d.). Mission Bible Class. https://missionbibleclass.org/new-testament/part2/acts-the-church-begins/paul-saul-becomes-a-christian/

Schmidt, T. (n.d.). *Five ways to start relying on God's promises.* Tyndale. https://www.tyndale.com/sites/unfoldingfaithblog/2019/06/20/five-ways-to-start-relying-on-gods-promises/

Seymour, D. (2020, September 8). *It is time to wake up from your slumber.* The Sun. https://suntci.com/it-is-time-to-wake-up-from-your-slumber-p5393-129.htm

Shields, J. (2022, September 25). *The story of God and man part 2: The fall.* Stonebrook Church. https://stonebrook.org/resources/sermons/the-story-of-god-and-man-the-fall

Simone, N. (n.d.). *How to have a quiet time with God (&Why it's important).* Be In Not Of. https://beinnotof.com/post/quiet-time-how-to

Sivonen, M. (2024, April 21). *The Shepherd among his sheep.* The Gospel Coalition. https://norden.thegospelcoalition.org/article/the-shepherd-among-his-sheep/

Skarp, M. (2011, March 30). *Learning from Jesus' prayer in the garden.* Berean Baptist Church. https://www.bereanmn.com/berean-blog/learning-from-jesus-prayer-in-the-garden/

Slattery, J. (2021, March 11). *When God calls us back to where we've failed.* JenniferSlatteryLivesOutLoud. https://jenniferslatterylivesoutloud.com/2021/03/11/when-god-calls-us-back-to-where-weve-failed/

Smith, B. (2021, February 9). *God's precious possession.* Metanoia Prison Ministries. https://www.metanoiaprisonministries.org/barry-smith/gods-precious-possession

Smith, C. (2018, May 3). *Seven ways Christ is the good shepherd.* Open The Bible. https://openthebible.org/article/seven-ways-christ-is-the-good-shepherd/

The soap method. (n.d.). Love God Greatly. https://lovegodgreatly.com/how-to-soap/

Sobogun, O. (2021, August 26). *Failure is not the end of Gods plan.* On Mission. https://onmission.uk/failure-is-not-the-end-of-gods-plan/

Soehnlin, J. (2016, September 24). *What it means to trust the good shepherd.* Embracing Life. https://embracing.life/article/trusting-shepherd-life-hard

Staney, B. (n.d.). God's promises: 50+ powerful Bible promises to build your faith. *Compassion.* https://www.compassionuk.org/blogs/gods-promises/

Staying spiritually alert. (2020, October 26). Devotions by Chris. https://devotionsbychris.com/2020/10/26/staying-spiritually-alert/

Stewart, M. (n.d.). *How can I truly align myself with God's will?* The Church of Jesus Christ of Latter-Day Saints. https://www.churchofjesuschrist.org/study/liahona/2024/04/digital-only-young-adults/how-can-i-truly-align-myself-with-gods-will?lang=eng

Stier, G. (2023, April 4). *The unimaginable suffering of Jesus.* Greg Stier. https://gregstier.org/the-unimaginable-suffering-of-jesus/

Stone, C. (2019, June 24). 7 things that are true when we run from God. *Outreach Magazine.* https://outreachmagazine.com/features/discipleship/43811-7-things-that-are-true-when-we-run-from-god.html

Straying away from God—Sin after salvation. (n.d.). Abiding Walk. https://www.abidingwalk.com/straying-away-from-god-sin-after-salvation/

Sunday, D. (2019, June 19). *How to fight when you fail.* Desiring God. https://www.desiringgod.org/articles/how-to-fight-when-you-fail

Swartzentruber, S. (2011, January 18). *The sheep of God's pasture.* Banner. https://www.thebanner.org/departments/2011/01/the-sheep-of-god-s-pasture

Tautges, P. (2023, March 23). *Counsel the bitter person with a warning from Jesus.* Assiociation of Certified Biblical Counselors. https://biblicalcounseling.com/resource-library/articles/counsel-the-bitter-person-with-a-warning-from-jesus/

Taylor, B. (2018, October 15). If humility is so important, why are leaders so arrogant? *Harvard Business Review.* https://hbr.org/2018/10/if-humility-is-so-important-why-are-leaders-so-arrogant

10 tips to improve your devotional life. (n.d.). King's Chruch International. https://kcionline.org/10-tips-to-improve-your-daily-devotional

TerKeurst, L. (2019, July 11). *When giving grace feels hard.* Proverbs 31. https://proverbs31.org/read/devotions/full-post/2019/07/11/when-giving-grace-feels-hard

Thomas, S. (2013, September 26). *The good shepherd | John 10: 1–21.* City Harvest AG Church. https://cityharvestag.com/sermons/jesus-the-good-shepherd/

Thompson, J. (2021, September 15). *What can we learn from each time Peter denies Jesus?* Crosswalk.com. https://www.crosswalk.com/faith/bible-study/what-can-we-learn-from-each-time-peter-denied-jesus.html

Trunnel, J. (2020, February 12). *Learning from the solitude of Jesus.* A Scriptured Life. https://ascripturedlife.com/2020/02/12/learning-from-the-solitude-of-jesus/

Tucker, L. (2024, March 5). *What is the story of Job?* Christianity.com. https://www.christianity.com/wiki/bible/what-is-the-story-of-job.html

25 ways to be closer to God. (n.d.). *Life Beautiful Magazine.* https://lifebeautifulmagazine.com/faith/25-ways-to-be-closer-to-god

Understanding discipleship. (2023, February 10). Global Disciples. https://www.globaldisciples.ca/blog/conditions-of-discipleship/

Understanding the role of the Holy Spirit as our helper. (n.d.). Beautiful in Jesus. https://beautifulinjesus.com/holy-spirit-helper/

Van Dyke, Z. (2020, January 27). *I am the Good Shepherd.* Man in the Mirror. https://maninthemirror.org/2020/01/27/i-am-the-good-shepherd/

Waiting on God: the virtue of persistence in the Christian journey. (n.d.). Shalom. https://shalomfortheworld.com/waiting-on-god-the-virtue-of-persistence-in-the-christian-journey/

Ward, S. (n.d.). *Surrender is a choice.* Steps. https://lifeimprovementsteps.com/surrender-is-a-choice/

Ware, P. (2021, February 4). *Finding Jesus: Reaching for God, nit substitutes.* Heartlight. https://www.heartlight.org/articles/202102/20210204_godshapedhole.html

Webb, C. (n.d.). *Becoming like Jesus: compassionate life.* Renovaré. https://renovare.org/articles/becoming-like-jesus-compassionate-life

WebMD Editorial Contributor. (n.d.). *Health benefits of running.* WebMD. https://www.webmd.com/fitness-exercise/health-benefits-running

Wells, S. M. (n.d.). *Stay alert and walk with your God.* God Hears Her. https://godhearsher.org/blog/stay-alert-and-walk-with-your-god/

What does it mean that the Lord is my Shepherd (Psalm 23)? (n.d.). Got Questions. https://www.gotquestions.org/Lord-is-my-Shepherd.html

What does it mean to be in Christ? (n.d.). Got Questions. https://www.gotquestions.org/in-Christ.html

What does Phillippians 3:9 mean? (n.d.). BibleRef. https://www.bibleref.com/Philippians/3/Philippians-3-9.html

What God says when you feel like a failure. (2020, August 4). Boldly Rise. https://boldlyrise.com/bold-faith/learning-to-be-bold/what-god-says-when-you-feel-like-a-failure/

What is spiritual discernment? It's signs and power explained. (n.d.). Pray.com. https://www.pray.com/articles/what-is-spiritual-discernment-its-signs-and-power-explained

When it's hard to give grace. (n.d.). Neue Thing. https://neuething.org/when-its-hard-to-give-grace/

Why are Christians called sheep? (2022, March 4). International Leadership Institute. https://iliteam.org/coreleadership/why-are-christians-called-sheep

Why believes face storms. (2022, September 11). Hallstorm Heart and Home. https://www.hallstromheartandhome.com/why-believers-face-storms

Why did God make salvation such a narrow path? (n.d.). Got Questions. https://www.gotquestions.org/narrow-path.html

Wild, M. (2019, July 9). *Encountering Jesus changes everything.* Mel Wild. https://melwild.wordpress.com/2019/07/09/encountering-jesus/

Williams, J. (2020, April 27). *God hasn't set you up to fail.* Proverbs31. https://proverbs31.org/read/devotions/full-post/2020/04/27/god-hasnt-set-you-up-to-fail

Wingate, K. (2024, July 16). *God knows where you are.* Proverbs31. https://proverbs31.org/read/devotions/full-post/2024/07/16/god-knows-where-you-are

The work of the good shepherd (John 10:1–16)—Mark Ottaway. (2023, October 1). Elim Bible Chapel. https://elimbiblechapel.com/2023/10/01/the-work-of-the-good-shepherd-john-101-16-mark-ottaway/

You may have failed—but God is not done with you. (n.d.). Wayne Stiles. https://www.waynestiles.com/blog/yes-you-failed-but-god-is-not-done-with-you/

Printed in Great Britain
by Amazon